D1442474

THE GREAT
SAN FRANCISCO
EARTHQUAKE AND FIRE, 1906

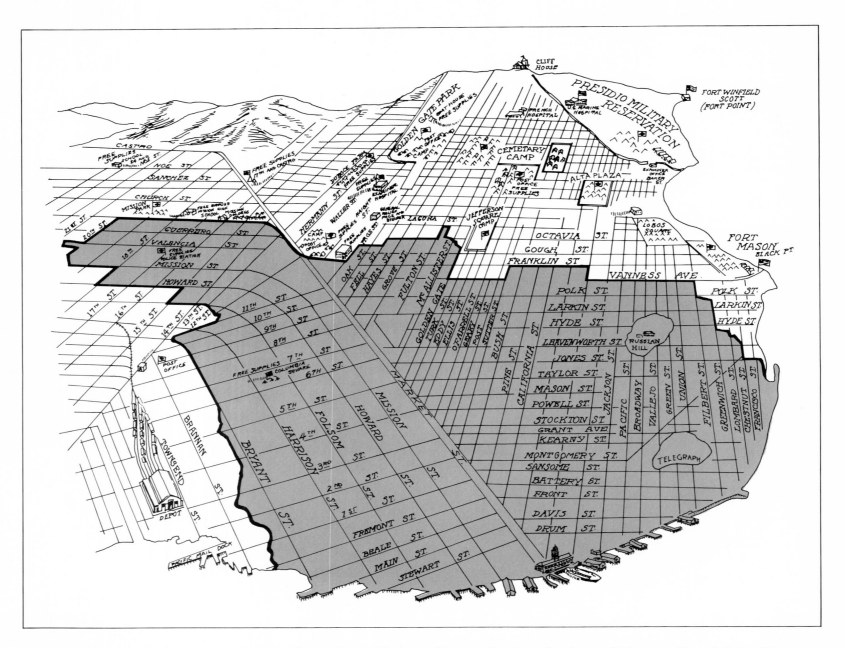

The burned district of San Francisco is shown within the heavy black lines, the general boundaries being the water front from Brannan street on the east to Jones street on the north, thence along Jones to Chestnut, to Hyde, to Polk, to Filbert, to Van Ness Avenue, to Clay, to Franklin, to Sutter, to Van Ness Avenue, to Golden Gate Avenue, to Octavia, to Page, to Gough, to Market, to Dolores, to Twentieth, to Mission, to Eighteenth, to Howard, to Fifteenth, to Folsom, to Bryant, to the water front. This map originally appeared in the pamphlet *San Francisco and Vicinity: Before and After the Big Fire*, published in 1906 by Rieder, Cardinell & Company.

THE GREAT
SAN FRANCISCO
EARTHQUAKE AND
FIRE, 1906

ERIC SAUL
DON DENEVI

CELESTIAL ARTS
MILLBRAE, CALIFORNIA

FOR OUR PARENTS
ALDO AND ADELE DENEVI
MILTON AND MARTHA SAUL

Celestial Arts
231 Adrian Road
Millbrae, CA 94030

First Printing, February, 1981

Designed by Abigail Johnston
Composition by HMS Typography
Printed by George Lithograph
Bound by Roswell Bookbinding

Manufactured in the United States of America

Library of Congress Cataloging in Publication Data

Saul, Eric.
The San Francisco earthquake and fire 1906.

Includes index.
1. San Francisco—Earthquake and fire, 1906.
I. DeNevi, Donald P., joint author. II. Title.
QE535.2.U6S28   979.4'61051   80-83616
ISBN 0-89087-288-0

1 2 3 4 5 6 7   86 85 84 83 82 81 80

CONTENTS

ACKNOWLEDGEMENTS

The authors would like to thank Gladys Hansen, Director of the Archives and History Room, San Francisco Public Library, who has dedicated so much of her time to preserving the records of the city's history. Without her careful and loving work, many of the photographs reproduced here may never have emerged in print. An additional thanks to Patricia Akre, photograph curator, for her assistance. Unless otherwise credited, the photographs in this book are from the San Francisco Library's collection.

Our thanks also to Lawrence Dinnean, Curator of Pictorial Collection, Bancroft Library; Leroy D. Wiems, photographic services, University of California Library, Berkeley; Nancy Crawford; Michael R. Green; Kim Combs, Assistant Director, Presidio Army Museum; J. Eduard Green, Curator of Collections, Presidio Army Museum; and Mary Russel.

*Again and again in California, great Nature, the mystic world-
mother, has sounded the note sublime. Seashore, desert,
mountain, giant tree, strange valley, towering cliff — all
have been staged for a world spectacle, a drama of
magnificence. But Her greatest work was the
carving out of Golden Hills a radiant blue
bay. Now comes modern man to nestle
around it a white city, a city of hope,
miracles and highest aspirations.*
EDWIN MARKHAM

The Midwinter Fair of 1894, Golden Gate Park.

ONE

THE CITY THAT WAS

FROM HER EARLIEST BEGINNINGS, CALIFORNIA, and her stunning geographical setting, the bay of San Francisco, has been steeped in romance. For over two centuries, Spanish galleons laid their courses from Manila to Cape Mendocino, then skirted the Californias, past what was to be the port of Saint Francis, on their way south to Panama and around the southern tip of South America. The route was well-known to Sir Francis Drake, the plunderer of Spanish ships and settlements, who used a bay north of the Golden Gate to repair and provision the *Golden Hind* before crossing the Pacific and circumnavigating the globe.

Two hundred years later, in 1776, the city of Saint Francis was founded by the Spanish even as the American Union was being forged on the opposite coast. It was the Franciscan order, building the chain of missions of Junipero Serra, along with the Spanish government represented by Juan Bautista de Anza, who founded the settlement, then called Yerba Buena. In 1846, a U.S. naval force took the town. In 1847 it was renamed San Francisco. After the discovery of gold in 1848, the town of 800 grew to a vibrant city of 25,000 by 1850, the year California joined the Union.

After the first golden nugget was found, thousands upon thousands flocked into an area that was the gateway to interior California. Year after year, they came from the east, north, and south, and even from the distant west, China, to test the promise of the Golden Gate. Many came to this fledgling city of the west for the simple climactic pleasures. Most, however, alert and sensing the future, arrived to bend their backs to earn the rewards awaiting them.

By 1900, the city of San Francisco had begun to realize its destiny. From a small cluster of bayside shacks huddled in the lee of sheltering hills, the city had rapidly grown into a complex community. Close beneath her forty-four hills, a fascinating harbor had already grown to rank among the five finest in the United States. Here the rails of the great transcontinental roads, the Southern Pacific and the Santa Fe, met water at the edge of a bay where there was room for every ship in the world to find shelter at one time. It had become the financial capital of the west with not only major banks represented but also the Stock Exchange, the U.S. Mint, and the Subtreasury having buildings in the city. It was one of the most cosmopolitan cities to be found anywhere with large enclaves of Chinese, Italians, and Irish. San Francisco was the focus for the most concentrated population in the west with half of the people in California living within easy reach of the Bay. Situated in the midst of unlimited natural resources with a climate that featured only 20 inches of rain a year and no snow, it was not astonishing that by the turn of the century, San Francisco was the headquarters for the leading financial, railroad, shipping, lumber, manufacturing, and distribution interests of the whole West Coast. And, its free-wheeling, open attitude attracted the most creative and enthusiastic people of the age.

In 1892, America's first gasoline automobile chugged down a street. Although the automobile's future was far from assured, the first shipment arrived the very next year at San Francisco's Pier 29. By April of 1898, Admiral Dewey was overwhelming the Spanish fleet in the Philippines; ships were carrying men from Seattle, Portland, and San Francisco to Skagway, Alaska, to cash in on the Klondike gold rush; Hawaii became a U.S. territory; and Californians, San Franciscans in particular, looked forward optimistically to the coming of a new century and the better, more modern world it was sure to bring.

A Victory Parade down Market Street signals the end of the Spanish-American War. San Francisco at the turn of the century had become the jumping off point for America's imperialistic adventures at annexing land in the Pacific.

By 1900, California led all other states in agriculture as well as petroleum productivity. From the Napa, San Joaquin, and Santa Clara Valleys, grapes, fruits, vegetables, and nuts poured forth, supplying the nation's food baskets. And, less than three years later, the first New York-to-San Francisco automobile drive took place. There was little question about it, out of a spirited, pioneer past there had come a present whose force was dynamic.

The era between 1890 and 1905 was a period of growth, expansion, and innovation in San Francisco. Real estate dealers estimated that between 3,000 and 5,000 new people were arriving every month. The spirit of expansion and ingenuity was particularly felt in the areas of shipping, technology, communication, and transportation. San Francisco was slowly being lit up with electricity, telephones came into wide use, and the wireless radio was on the horizon; even the miracle of Thomas Edison's motion pictures was but a short step away.

Men of vision looked inland to the valleys lying at the foot of the Sierra and their incredibly productive soils where a few hundred thousand people were scattered. These handfuls could feed millions with the soil they worked. Seaward, businessmen scrutinized the unlimited possibilities of trade with four hundred million Asians. In the contest for the trade of the Orient, San Francisco had the advantage of position. The only requirements needed for the building of huge personal empires were energy and seed money. And, neither of these were to be found wanting. More and larger steamers were sent off to trade, while the wharf rooms of the city were strained to handle the growth of traffic. Soon, some of the largest steamers in the world were being built in Bay shipyards in order to accommodate the goods flowing between the Golden Gate and Asiatic ports. San Francisco quickly became not only the warehouse, but the marketplace of a state unsurpassed in mineral wealth and agriculture.

The opening months of 1906 promised that in every area business profits would surpass those of the preceding year. New buildings were projected and talk of a "Big City" was crystallizing into a "Greater Golden Gate and San Francisco" movement. By April 1906, construction for both business and residence was going on at an astounding rate. The business district had been enlarging its borders since 1895 as old structures were torn down and new buildings took their places. Great blocks of business buildings were erected in the wholesale districts, and more were rising as fast as the workmen could put them up. In the residential districts, the building boom was even more dramatic. Never had so many homes been thrown up so quickly. Generally, these ranged from five-room flats to hundred-room family hotels. And yet, the demand outran the supply. In 1900, there had been over 50,000 houses in the city; six years later there were over 85,000.

On the top of Nob Hill, Crocker, Colton, Huntington, Hopkins, and Stanford built their monument mansions. These baronial castles epitomized the extravagance and conspicuous consumption of the mid-19th century — their 50-to-70 rooms resembling Victorian art museums rather than comfortable quarters in which to live.

Through the Golden Gate and to these docks came trading ships from all over the world. These brick warehouses at the foot of Telegraph Hill survived the temblors of April 18, 1906; the warehouse district and many wharves also survived the fire that followed because firemen could pump water from the Bay onto the burning buildings.

Facing page. This view from Russian Hill at the corner of Taylor and Green Streets was photographed on April 6, 1906. Twelve days later, this neighborhood was destroyed, along with many similar modest, middle-class neighborhoods throughout the city.

In 1900, the city government had finally moved into the new City Hall, a ponderous monument that had been begun in 1871. It was the most obvious symbol of transition from one corrupt city government to another. For an entire generation, the construction firm of Shea and Shea regularly supplied a return for the city officials who allowed the continuing increased costs of erecting the building, from an estimated $2,000,000 to as much as $8,000,000 on completion. This example of boodling was by no means an isolated situation, but was particularly representative of the accepted means of doing business in San Francisco. Despite its reputation, in 1906 the City Hall's lofty dome offered an imposing appearance of which most citizens were proud.

A large number of theaters could be found scattered throughout the city, the most notable being the Grand Opera House on Mission near the Palace Hotel. Other popular amusement spots included the Alcazar and the Orpheum on O'Farrell Street, the California on Bush Street, the Columbia on Powell Street, the Majestic on Market Street, the Tivoli on the corner of Eddy and Mason, and the famous Olympic Music Hall. San Francisco could also offer to both residents and tourists a Chinese temple which held weekly drama performances. And, as everyone knew, there were hundreds of smaller "music halls" on the Barbary Coast along Pacific Street, throughout North Beach, the Mission, and other areas, not to mention the "French" restaurants furnished with beds to complement the exotic meals.

8

The "temples of the money changers" were always architecturally imposing in the financial district; by April 1906, there were no less than 42 banks of all kinds. The religious temples of the city were counted at more than 170. The number of hotels had increased dramatically after the turn of the century and now included the Palace, the California, the St. Francis, the Occidental, the Lick, and the Russ.

Many of the residence hotels and private dwellings were built of wood, and fire warnings were issued regularly by the fire department. Builders had for many years faced a serious dilemma in San Francisco: Should buildings be constructed primarily of wood, which was much more able to withstand the earthquakes, but was hardly fireproof, or should "fireproof" buildings of brick or masonry and steel be built? A few were constructed of materials considered nonflammable, while many were built of redwood, assumed to be "slow-burning." The so-called fireproof buildings included the Appraisers' Warehouse, the *Call* (Spreckels) Building, the *Chronicle* Building, and the Crocker Building, among many others. These "safe" buildings averaged about eight stories, but a few attained skyscraper status of seventeen stories. The Merchants' Exchange and the Mills Building were constructed using the most modern engineering principles and materials and rivaled any skyscraper in the east. But the majority of buildings in the business district had been constructed from brick, stone, and wood. However, with virtually no exception, the tens of thousands of private residences in San Francisco had been built of redwood, not only because it was an inexpensive material, but also because of its supposed fire-resisting qualities.

For their "protection" from conflagration, the city's taxpayers paid dearly. But all agreed that the hundreds of thousands of dollars spent annually on their fire department would provide ample security. Although the fire department was acknowledged to be one of the best in the country, the premiums exacted by the insurance underwriters suggested they were not entirely convinced. A case in point appeared in the *Coast Review* of May 1906, quoting "eastern insurance men" as saying, "San Francisco is bound to burn down or up. It is a wooden city and someday fire will get beyond control of your fire department, excellent as it is." But still residents had little doubt that the 41 steam engines, nine trucks, seven "chemical" engines, and various monitor batteries and towers manned by a force of several hundred would be equal to any disaster. No one, not even in his wildest imagination, predicted an uncontrollable conflagration. Citizens had observed the fire department deal with numerous major blazes, such as that which destroyed the Baldwin Hotel, and the one which gutted the Bancroft History Publications building (which contained the largest stock of books on the West Coast) back in 1904. People had also watched the containment of various menacing fires along the waterfront. No, there was little question about it, San Francisco had one of the most modern, efficient, and able fire teams anywhere, and citizens had perfect confidence in their ability to cope with any emergency.

The "temples of the money changers" along California Street, looking east from Kearny, and a look west towards Nob Hill crowned by the Fairmont Hotel, completed in 1904.

The California Hotel on Bush Street. Next door is the Bush Street fire house where Fire Chief Dennis Sullivan lived as well as worked.

The St. Francis Hotel, built in 1904, on Union Square in the heart of downtown. The square was named during the Civil War, but the monument at its center is dedicated to Admiral George Dewey, a hero of the Spanish-American War.

Kearny Street, looking south from Sutter toward the *Call*-Spreckels Building.

Market Street — the main thoroughfare of San Francisco. The south side of Market, between Third and Fourth, 1905. Market was called "the Slot" because of the cable slots between the tracks in the middle of the street. The working-class and industrial district south of Market was called "south of the slot." *Facing page. Upper left.* Looking west on Market, July, 1905. *Lower left.* Market just 18 days before the earthquake. *Upper right.* The grand (and "fire-proof") Palace Hotel. *Lower right.* "Newspaper Row," the intersection of Market, Third, and Kearny, the location of Hearst's *Examiner,* the *Call*-Spreckles Building, the *Chronicle,* and the *Daily News.*

Looking west out Market Street, left, and O'Farrell Street, right, from
the *Call*-Spreckels Building, May 27, 1900.

On Tuesday, April 17, 1906, thoughts of disaster were far from the minds of the people of San Francisco. Things couldn't have been better for the continuing growth and development of the city. The population, which had been 342,782 in 1900, was now approaching the 500,000 mark. The changes in the past five and a half years were considered small compared to those that were about to occur during the next decade. Everyone believed that the coming ten-year span, to be topped off with the International Panama-Pacific Exposition, would bring more prosperity, innovation, and growth than had occurred over the past forty years put together. San Francisco was in excellent condition. Despite the corrupt city government, she was young, vigorous, and dynamic.

On that night, many San Franciscans were enjoying the second night of the opera season. Filling the city's Grand Opera House from pit to dome, the audience heard *Carmen* starring Enrico Caruso and Olive Fremstad. Monday evening's performance of *The Queen of Sheba* had been subjected to a rather scathing set of reviews from the local critics. Caruso took the criticism to heart and castigated the cast, many of them local performers, to rise above this lacklusterness and throw themselves into tonight's fiery roles. Unfortunately, Madame Fremstad, a famed Wagnerian diva, was indignant with Caruso as well as the critics. And only minutes prior to curtain was conductor Alfred Hertz able to mollify the temperamental artists and entreat them to bring their best to the performance.

Enrico Caruso as Don Jose in Bizet's *Carmen*, which he sang to a full house on the evening of April 17, 1906. Caruso, greatly shaken and terrified by the earthquake, fled San Francisco vowing never to return — a promise which he kept.

17

Elected mayor of San Francisco in 1901, Eugene Schmitz was the graft-ridden, boodling pawn of political boss Abe Ruef who had literally plucked him out of the orchestra pit of the Columbia Theatre. Considered weak and ineffectual by many, Schmitz rose to the occasion to become an able and capable administrator during the tragic days following the earthquake and fire. On the eve of April 18, 1906, little did he know that an investigation of corruption in the Mayor's office was underway.

After listening to a thrilling performance, particularly that of Caruso, many opera aficionados crowded fashionable restaurants. However, other San Franciscans were busy at more serious activities. That same night, civic reformers met to wrestle with the problems of corruption in the city's administration. The primary targets were Mayor Eugene Schmitz and Boss Abraham Ruef. Ruef had hand-picked Schmitz, just as he had selected the 18 supervisors elected the year before at the time of the mayor's reelection for a third term. Ruef had also chosen the district attorney, William A. Langdon, but in so doing, had overlooked one of Langdon's character traits—he was honest.

Millionaire Adolph Spreckels had put up $100,000 to support the campaign against the corrupt officials and *Bulletin* editor Fremont Older, former mayor James Phelan, detective William J. Burns, and Francis J. Heney from Oregon formed the upper echelon of a group that would eventually doom the political graft that permeated city government. While each of these men would have insisted, Tuesday evening, that corruption was the most serious problem facing the people of San Francisco, within hours they would be joining forces with the same officials they were intent on condemning to deal with an even greater, and more immediate problem.

Van Ness Avenue, looking south from Hayes Street, 1905. Note the campaign poster for Eugene Schmitz.

TWO

THE EARTHQUAKED . . . IT GROANED ALOUD IN AGONY

THE SAN FRANCISCO OF EARLY 1906 was as exciting a place to be as could be found around the world . . . and as wide open. Missionary Mary McDermitt of the Flying Rollers of the House of David, early in that year, had condemned the city to be destroyed in an earthquake, a condemnation the citizenry ignored as blithely as they had her efforts to recruit them to her sect. Other efforts to "save" the frolicking cosmopolis were treated with equal disdain . . . but perhaps Sister McDermitt had contacts in higher places. . . .

San Franciscans of 1906 were familiar with earthquakes, at least with those that rattle windows and china cabinets, but do little, if any, noticeable damage. Over two hundred temblors had been recorded in northern California between 1850 and 1886, with most of them occurring around San Francisco Bay. However, during the first months of 1906, there was diminished activity and for the first sixteen days of April none at all. And, according to a U.S. Geological Survey report published in 1907, "It is fair to assume, therefore, that the great earthquake resulted from an accumulation of stresses which would ordinarily have been relieved by smaller movements."

There is nothing so singularly shattering to the serenity and self-confidence of a city as when the ground strains its thin coat and bursts its seams, spewing forth sudden destruction. San Francisco refused to learn the lessons of its past history. During its previous 140-year history, the San Francisco Bay area had suffered a number of devastating earthquakes. Of these, the earliest large shock known occurred in June of 1836 along the Hayward Fault and may have had a magnitude of more than 8.0 on the Richter Scale. The next severe shock in late June 1838 occurred on the San Andreas Fault in the foothills west of Palo Alto. This temblor was also compared in magnitude to the June 1836 quake. At this early date, the San Francisco business district was called Yerba Buena and consisted of not more than eight or ten simple wooden structures and the immediate area had no more than 60 or 70 people. In 1865, another 8+ earthquake hit somewhere in the hills south of San Francisco. Three years later, the young metropolis was rocked again by a severe earthquake. With 12 people killed and over $400,000 in property damage, the shock is estimated to have had a magnitude of 7.5.

San Francisco had a long history and reputation of "self incendiary tendencies." Six disastrous fires destroyed most of the city between December 1849 and June 1851. In 1865, San Francisco experienced a major earthquake and another followed three years later. While one artist viewed the 1865 quake with a certain morbid humor, builders began thinking seriously about different construction methods. After the two big temblors, wood started to replace brick as a building material as it was thought to have "give"—buildings made of it would sway very much like trees in the wind whereas rigid brick structures would crack and crumble. By 1906, most of the homes in San Francisco were constructed of wood.

Of course, the most significant earthquake in the history of the Bay area in terms of lives lost and property damage was the great earthquake of April 18, 1906. Early that morning, the San Andreas Fault once again yielded to the earth's accumulated pressure. For years, deep in the earth, perhaps as far down as twelve miles, fearful and little understood forces were at work on the earth's crust, twisting and straining the great layers of rock. That morning, at approximately twelve minutes past five at a point called the epicenter, the rock gave way, snapping and shifting in an instant with an approximate force of 12,000 Hiroshima-size atomic explosions, the equivalent of 6,000,000 tons of TNT. The devastation spread with terrible speed along a 270-mile corridor from Point Arena in the north, all the way south to Hollister and Salinas. Incredible displacements of up to 25 feet were immediately recognizable and the temblor was felt as far away as 400 miles in such towns and cities as Coos Bay in Oregon, Winnemucca in Nevada, and Los Angeles. The sudden shock severed water mains in San Francisco, Santa Rosa, and Fort Ross, depriving firefighting units of their necessary water supplies.

The entire San Francisco peninsula began to tremble as the quake centered somewhere near Woodside, twenty miles south of the Golden Gate. The steady shaking lasted, according to the most reliable reports, a total of 28 seconds and, although the Richter scale was not developed until some 30 years later, had an estimated magnitude of more than 8.0. It was the greatest earthquake ever recorded along the San Andreas Fault, a XI on the Mercalli Intensity Scale: "Few, if any (masonry), structures remain standing. Bridges destroyed. Broad fissures in ground. Underground pipelines completely out of surface. Earth slumps and land slips in soft ground. Rails bent greatly."

Crackling through the earth at thousands of miles an hour, the shock wave sliced, churned, and ruptured the San Francisco peninsula like some enormous disc harrow drawn over the surface. Jolting San Franciscans into instant terror, the entire city of San Francisco rocked as the ground rippled and swelled. Accompanied by a roar which sounded like a thousand freight trains out of control, streets and avenues billowed with the upward thrust of the shock, shaking and pitching the few pedestrians and horse-drawn carts which happened to be out at that hour. Downtown buildings began to shudder and sway, loosening cascades of glass, ornamental stonework, and granite. Huge hunks of office buildings were shaken loose by the tons within the first few seconds of violent vibration. The entire San Francisco skyline rocked like a huge clipper in a hurricane. Cheap brick structures disintegrated by the score, as their interiors became maelstroms of flying dishes, bookshelves, and wall hangings.

Twisted cable car tracks on Union Street and a wide fissure on 18th Street. Such extreme earth movements were common in areas of land fill, underground stream beds, and water department installations.

ARNOLD GENTHE/BANCROFT LIBRARY

A LOW, *rumbling noise, a savage succession of twists, a rocking motion to the south and north, a cessation of an instant and now the twist and the shake, as of the earth in agony, and then the monstrous quake and the low rumbling noise like the fluttering of wings of steel, dying away to nothing, followed by a silence so keen that all nature seemed to stop to listen. This was the minor chord to the great smash and clash of groaning buildings, the creaking of battered walls, the snapping of steel, the cracking of glass and the shrieks of dying men. The cries of the wounded were mingled with those of frightened horses, frightened into speech, to call out in horrid unaccustomed tones the affright of all things that live. The earth quaked and rocked and heaved and rolled and swelled and, aye, it groaned aloud in agony.* PIERRE N. BERINGER

25

IF there had to be an earthquake, no more desirable hour could have been selected. Even in San Francisco, which was formerly noted as an "all night" town, there are but few people on the streets at 5 o'clock in the morning. It was too late for the night reveller to be abroad, and too early for the good citizens to be out of bed. Consequently, when chimneys toppled into the streets, and cornices and facade ornaments, and portions of flimsy walls came crashing down, but few people on the streets were injured. The loss of life occurred mainly in old ramshackle frame buildings that collapsed and crushed their inmates. The exact number of these unfortunates will never be known. PAUL COWLES

Neighborhood residents and a San Francisco building inspector assessing the damage along Howard Street, between 17th and 18th. These buildings survived the fire and became popular postcard images, but whether the rooms to let were equally popular is unknown.

During the earthquake, thousands of brick chimneys toppled and crashed through roofs, injuring or killing hundreds. Damaged and spark-leaking chimneys that did not topple were the cause of many terrible fires that started in the morning hours following the quake. The usual occupant of this bed was fortunate to be somewhere else at the time of the upheaval.

27

Sightseeing, gawking, and posing for pictures were popular pasttimes in the early morning hours of April 18. Behind the collapsed buildings on Golden Gate Avenue and Hyde rises the dome of the Hall of Records.

29

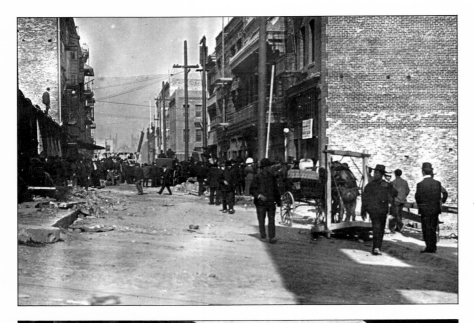

Less than 30 seconds had elapsed since the first jolt was felt, but everywhere there was unbelievable agony and destruction. While the shock waves were still being felt, fires began erupting everywhere. Firefighters had quickly scrambled into action, but their trucks could not negotiate the torn-up streets. Because of broken water mains, fire hydrants were useless. Meanwhile, dust- and smoke-blinded pedestrians who survived the initial shock milled about the toppled buildings and brick-piled avenues in stunned horror.

Everyone living through those endless seconds knew that the city was enduring a tremendous ordeal, and those who were not too terrified, after the vibrations ceased, began to investigate the extent of Nature's rage. As the streets in the residential districts were being filled with hastily attired people aroused from their early morning sleep, more than fifty small fires began. Gas connections had broken, electric wires had crossed, chimneys had fallen, stoves had overturned, and countless combustible jars of chemicals had toppled from drugstore shelves.

Most of the buildings in Chinatown, composed of brick and masonry, suffered severe damage during the quake, what was left burned to the ground soon after. The movement to rebuild Chinatown on the outskirts of the city was unsuccessful.

31

I WAS *awakened at 5:13 on the bright sunny morning of April 18th . . . and enjoyed the wheezy undulations of the house, which mark the usual harmless California earthquake. The wave which woke (me) was gentle enough, but the next one, like the bump of an express train, seemed a little severe. But it was a straight wave and harmed nothing. Then the* temblor *began to take hold. The bedroom on the second floor swayed like a ship in a hurricane. A lantern standing in the hall leaped in through the open door. Pictures swayed, earthenware leaped about. Some mighty force seemed to hold the house, and to be trying to whip the ground with it.*

. . . this was the REAL THING. And it seemed to be over-done. A California earthquake was due to last for a few seconds only, but this did not know when to stop. Now the power was trying to twist the house about its chimneys, taking each of the three in turn. I rushed along the reeling gangway of the house, seized the baby and got out on the veranda, where bricks could not fall. The older boy, who was sleeping on the roof, clung on as to a runaway horse. As things became a little calmer he shouted down: "The church is falling! The gymnasium is caving in! Everything has gone bum!" I saw the dust of mortar rising, and the students crowding in the roads, and then I knew that we had had an epoch-marking earthquake. DAVID STORR JORDAN

The spires of St. Dominic's Church on Fillmore in the Western Addition faired very poorly. Across the street two men sit reading, comfortable and blasé on a piece of fallen decorative woodwork.

Awakened from a sound sleep to find myself in the midst of falling plaster, breaking glass and flying furniture, and to hear the thunder-like roar of falling walls, escape, indeed, seemed impossible.

. . . Market street, the famous thoroughfare of the Western metropolis was . . . torn and broken, curved, cut and twisted, the evidence of the force exerted by nature in this monster wrecking was almost unbelievable. Street carsrails were buckled and con-torted. Big fissures had permitted the salt water to be forced up from below; for this section of the city was "made" ground. The danger of its sinking into the bay should another quake attack it, was vividly apparent. The very air was charged with danger. Frightened people were pouring from every building. All were breathlessly awaiting another shock. When it came, the heart seemed to stand still—but it passed, a slight and harmless one.   F. O. POPENOE

33

Between 30 and 80 people lost their lives when the four-story Valencia Hotel collapsed in the Mission district. It was the greatest single tragedy that occured as a result of the quake. Many victims, trapped in the wreckage, were drowned when water from a burst main flooded the basement. Before the fires began, volunteers picked through the jumbled remains in search of survivors.

Right away it was incredible—the violence of the quake. It started with a directness, a savage determination that left no doubt of its purpose . . . First, for a few seconds a feeling of incredulity, capped immediately with one of finality—of incredulity at the violence of the vibrations. "It's the end—St. Pierre, Samoa, Vesuvius, Formosa, San Francisco—this is death." Simultaneously with that, a picture of the city swaying beneath the curl of a tidal wave foaming to the sky. . . .

I got up and walked to the window. I started to open it, but the pane obligingly fell outward and I poked my head out, the floor like a geyser beneath my feet. Then I heard the roar of bricks coming down in cataracts and the groaning of twisted girders all over the city, and at the same time I saw the moon, a calm, pale crescent in the green sky of dawn. . . .

Just then the quake, with a sound as of a snarl, rose to its climax of rage, and the back wall of my building for three stories above me fell . . . It struck some little wooden houses in the alley below. I saw them crash in like emptied eggs and the bricks pass through the roof as through tissue paper.

. . . Throughout the long quaking, in this great house full of people (the Neptune Hotel on Post Street) I had not heard a cry, not a sound, not a sob, not a whisper. And now, when the roar of crumbling buildings was over and only a brick was falling here and there like the trickle of a spent rain, this silence continued, and it was an awful thing. But now in the alley some one began to groan. It was a woman's groan, soft and low.

. . . the streets . . . were full of people, half-clad, dishevelled, but silent, absolutely silent, as if suddenly they had become speechless idiots . . . I went down Post Street toward the center of town, and in the morning's garish light I saw many men and women with gray faces, but none spoke. All of them, they had a singular hurt expression, not one of physical pain, but rather one of injured sensibilities, as if some trusted friend, say, had suddenly wronged them. . . . JAMES HOPPER

WALKING through beautiful Golden Gate Park on Tuesday afternoon, my two cousins, young women from Indiana, on their way home, said they had seen everything in California except an earthquake. When, just after 5:14 the next morning, I hurriedly dressed, I remarked to my roommate, Eugene Favre of the Call, that California had satisfied them now!

My roommate and I happened to be awake when the first shock came. In our third-story room of the four-story frame hotel, the St. Regis, a few blocks north of the City Hall (where I had been just two hours before), it sounded like the rush of a mighty tornado. As we lay in bed the house rocked like a ship in a heavy sea, a rising crescendo of storm, then a lull for a few moments, then stronger than before, an angry shake almost hurling us out upon the floor. Then subsidence. The earthquake was over. Before I left the room six more slight shocks had come, but they were nothing to one who had felt himself in the power of that first awful wrench!

As I passed among the rushing thousands on the streets, I had heard all sorts of rumors. "Los Angeles was burning up." "Seattle had sunk in the sea." "Chicago and New York were the prey of flames." "The whole country was tottering to ruin." These reports were believed by the terrified in the streets. As a newspaper man, I did not credit the rumors, but it seemed likely enough that the whole Pacific Coast had suffered the early morning shock.

WILLIAM H. THOMPSON

Private automobiles were pressed into service as ambulances during the emergency, and makeshift hospitals sprouted everywhere.

36

THE house swayed and creaked and trembled; rose and fell like a ship in a tempest. I couldn't walk on the floor at all—had to crawl to the door on my hands and knees. Just as I opened the door my big plaster cast of "The Winged Victory" fell from her pedestal and crashed on the floor. She made a big heap of rubbish. I was too terrified to think. I tried to call to the Dixons, but couldn't articulate. They didn't hear a sound from me throughout those terrible forty seconds. I thought it was the end—but neither the beautiful dreams nor the horrors that are supposed to panorama instant death came to me. My heart beat double quick somewhere up in my throat. I felt nauseated. But I managed to save my toppling mirror; saved it while all other breakable objects in my room went smash. I held on to it with one hand and braced myself against the door frame with the other and watched the crystal scent bottles slide off and spill their precious fragrance on the drunken floor; my statuette of Psyche fell from her shelf and broke her head off. But my little Aztec idol Huitzpochitle took his tumble like a valiant god-of-war without a scratch. He rolled about on the floor in a undignified way but he never changed expression. The final jerk almost upset the bureau on top of me, but after that my house rocked regularly for awhile like a swing when you "let the old cat die." I felt the ease which followed the cessation of great pain. . . .

In the Latin Quarter the streets were full of terrified people all crowding to keep in the middle of the street. It was the quietest crowd I was ever in. Scarcely any one spoke. The children didn't cry. The fear of God was upon us all. Everyone was afraid of another shock.   MARY EDITH GRISWOLD

37

THREE

THE CITY BURNED
WITH A COPPER GLOW . . .

THEN came the season of the awful silence, the hush of awe, when mankind held its breath and things stood still and humanity gazed on havoc and hideous horror and then, out of the silence, out of toppled buildings, ruined palaces, and dismal hovels, came the besom of flame. With hideous roar it advanced, this terrible thing, this red and yellow monster, and its fiery arms outstretched, it reached the seven hills and it hissed and roared and with infernal intensity, it consumed, ate, and devoured. Here it creeped along, a fawning thing, a fascinating though hideous snake and there it advanced boldly, compelling obedience by the sudden smash and relentless roar and rack of flame. One moment it subsided, the next it rose and flung itself upon all that it could consume in its mad fury. It followed the ground, it scaled the heights, it burned through steel and rock and then licked up wood as though it were straw. PIERRE N. BERINGER

FIRE CHIEF DENNIS SULLIVAN had just settled comfortably into sleep after returning from a warehouse fire near Market Street. The alarm had sounded just after midnight and Sullivan had left the firemen only after knowing the blaze was well in hand. In another bedroom, near the rear of the living quarters over the Bush Street fire house, Mrs. Sullivan slept soundly, used to the alarms, the comings and goings of the fire company. But at 5:12 that morning it was more than an alarm bell ringing, as she was jolted by the temblor and, simultaneously the ornamental roofing of the adjoining California Hotel began to crash through the firehouse and her bedroom, carrying her in her bed to the ground, three floors below. Miraculously, she was only slightly injured. But the Fire Chief, acting quickly to protect his wife, rushed into her bedroom only to be carried away with the bricks and rubble. He was removed from the debris only minutes later, but his injuries kept him in a coma during the period when his skills and experience were most needed. Sullivan died on Sunday morning, unaware of the Herculean task that had been required of his department.

40

Facing page. Looking down Geary Street at Stockton on Wednesday, April 18. Billows from the South-of-Market fire are seen behind the framework of the Whittell Building (under construction at the time of the quake) and the Palace Hotel

---

The "Ham-and-Eggs" fire burns in and around the ruins of City Hall and the Hall of Records. Before the end of the day, these buildings were destroyed and many official documents, deeds, certificates, and other important city records were lost.

From his quarters on Washington Street, Brigadier General Funston could look out over the downtown district. Within thirty minutes after the quake, he could see the smoke from fires on either side of Market Street:

Realizing from the intensity and duration of the shock that serious damage must have occurred, to say nothing of the resultant loss of life, (I) dressed and, finding that the street cars were not running, hastened on foot to the business part of the city . . . I noticed that columns of smoke were arising in various localities, particularly south of Market Street. Reaching Sansome, I saw that several fires were already burning fiercely in the banking district and that the firemen who were on the scene were quite owing to lack of water.

Already it was apparent that during the earthquake's half-minute duration, the main arterial conduits of the city's water system had been broken. Down the peninsula, one of the three pipelines ran directly over the San Andreas Fault for a distance of seven miles and was virtually destroyed. The other two main pipelines were broken at points where they crossed marshes. Within the city, the pipes of the distributing system were ruptured in those areas of filled ground, and where the financial district had been built.

General Frederick Funston gives instructions to his driver at Fort Mason.

An HOUR *after the shock, in the district between the Bay and Sansome Street, with rolling smoke above, and roaring, furious flames breathing hotly in our faces, I came upon a fire-engine from whose stack the smoke came faintly as from a kitchen chimney, and about which stood the firemen with idle hands.*

"For God's sake!"

"No water," said the Chief. "Mains all broken by the shock; can't do a thing."

"Dynamite!"

A shrug of the shoulders for reply. And not until an hour later did there come a resonant explosion that told that at least the fire was being fought, however futilely.

HENRY ANDERSON LAFLER

Left. The dome of City Hall is glimpsed through the smoke of the Hayes Valley fire. The curious gathered very close to the inferno, apparently unconcerned for their personal safety. The rubble in the street is the facade of a damaged house.

New York Mutual Life Building, California and Sansome Streets.

About an hour after the earthquake hit, the fire department sent an official along with a dozen or so firemen to the Presidio asking that explosives be made available. The artillerymen supplied 48 barrels of black powder, wire, and fuse loaded on the kit wagons of the field batteries. Two additional large wagons were quickly procured and loaded with the remaining powder and some 300 pounds of dynamite obtained from the city's engineering department. The powder and the dynamite were not the most desirable for the job at hand, but the needed stick dynamite could only be located on Angel Island. What they had on hand would have to do until the other arrived.

By nine that morning, as the fire spread to the southwest and the north, the whole population appeared cut off from escape to the east and north. A continuous line of flame seemed to extend from the north of Market Street, along the waterfront, past the Ferry Building, south of Market Street, and along Mission Street beyond Third Street where Southern Pacific's main railroad station was located.

The fire raged through the wholesale district, the retail and shopping areas, the chief financial centers, leading hotels and public buildings.

At 9:00 A.M., with an uncontrolled fire raging across the street on Montgomery, the first dynamiting of buildings began. Those dynamited were not more than three or four doors away from those already in flames. Early that morning, while preparations were being made for the destruction of the adjacent building, a fire was noticed raging in the

cellar of a store east of the Subtreasury on Commercial. Although efforts were made to put that fire out there was no water available and the fire soon engulfed the entire building. A structure between that fire and Kearny was then dynamited, but at that point, the small supply of stick dynamite, which had been supplied by the California Powder Works, ran out. A number of wagons then arrived loaded with giant powder—dynamite in granular form. The soldiers hesitated to use it, realizing that it had an active base, unsuited for this type of demolition because of its tendency to ignite combustible articles in the buildings being destroyed. But they received orders to use it anyway. The first building immediately caught on fire when the charge was detonated. The second, a cheap lodging house, also caught fire, but in that case, bits of bedding and clothing were ignited and thrown across Kearny, igniting that entire block.

During that first morning, the soldiers and volunteers fighting the fire often found that at certain points the wall of fire was outflanking them. Furthermore, the fires were merging into one huge fire rapidly approaching the Palace and Grand Hotels, the *Call*-Spreckels Building, Emporium, and other large buildings from the south.

The fire ruthlessly burns Meig's Wharf, located approximately where Pier 45 is on Fisherman's Wharf today.

47

THE SUN *was rising behind a smoky pall already floating above the populous district south of Market Street . . . At Tehama Street I saw the beginning of the fire which was to sweep all the district south of Market Street. It was swirling up the narrow way with a sound that was almost a scream. Before it the humble population of the district were fleeing, and in its path, as far as I could see, frail shanties went down like card houses . . . Over the tragedy the fire threw its flaming mantle of hypocrisy, and the full extent of the holocaust will never be known, will remain a poignant mystery.* JAMES HOPPER

Rescue efforts were abandoned as the fire approached the Valencia Hotel. Within hours, the fire would devour this Mission district neighborhood.

T WO BLOCKS *away, orange flames, tinged with the black of tar smoke, boiled from a tall gray building. One block away, a solitary automobile, three or four hurrying black figures of men with dynamite, an officer or two, all in the white brilliance of the flames; half a block away the building that had housed me, and nearer, sitting a white horse in the middle of the street, a cavalry-man keeping back the crowd.*

And that with difficulty. "They're going to dynamite!" he would cry; "Keep back, keep back!" And the sullen crowd moved back, all save a few who had prized possessions still a block and a half away from the licking, disastrous, red tongues. . . .

By ten o'clock, looking at the city from Telegraph Hill, which stands in the northeast corner of that finger of land upon which the city lies, one could discern a score of fires. East of Sansome, in the neighborhood of Clay, wholesale stores were all ablaze. South, towards Market, and near the ferry there were fires. The Grand Opera House was afire, and throughout the South-of-Market district, where were the homes of the poor, the fire was making its way.   HENRY ANDERSON LAFLER

The Mercantile Agency on the northeast corner of California and Sansome Streets.

Far right. The Appraiser's Building, the long brick structure just below the plume of smoke, appears to be threatened. However, this building and a few others in the immediate area (including the Montgomery Block and Hotaling's liquor warehouse) were eventually saved.

51

As the fire licks along Market Street to overtake the *Call*-Spreckels Building, the California National Guard and the United States Army enforce evacuation at bayonet point.

53

Arnold Genthe's famous view down Sacramento Street, Wednesday
April 18. This photograph has often been called one of the ten best news
photos of all times.

WE LIVED midway between Telegraph and Russian Hills, two of the highest points of the city, from either of which a wonderful view was obtained, and we climbed to the summit of the latter. Reaching there about a half an hour after the earthquake, we had our first idea of the awful scourge of fire that was to lay waste our beloved city. Meeting an acquaintance as we climbed, he said, "Look at the fires; the whole city will burn." We had passed some engines on their way to extinguish a fire at North Beach, where a huge gas tank had exploded, and we had noted a smaller fire near by, but the possibility of a general conflagration seemed too remote to be considered.

"Why, what nonsense," I said, "The whole city can't burn."

As we reached the crest of the hill, the man pointed. "See," he said, and from the northern shore of the city to the extreme south, from North Beach to the far end of the Mission, fires were blazing aloft. We counted twelve even then of sufficient size for a general alarm to be rung in by the department under ordinary circumstances.

"And the shock has broken the mains so that the water supply is shut off entirely," the man added grimly. "The city must burn." As we stood there silently we felt for the first time a definite premonition of the three awful days and nights to follow, the nerve-racking strain, the uncertainty, the bewilderment, the loss of life and property, the destruction of our dear city, the keen physical discomfort and the helplessness and terror caused by the slight but constantly recurring shocks of earthquake.

MARY ASHE MILLER

55

To present the advance of the fire in a sequential order is impossible. However, there was an effort on the part of the San Francisco *Chronicle* and its managing editor to cover every possible phase of the disaster. Gathering his force around him by 7:00 A.M., the editor ordered the reporters to especially check out the origins and extent of the fires then raging. He then went about his job of preparing an evening edition as if the earthquake and fire were nothing unusual. Within the hour, the reporters were piling eyewitness accounts on his desk.

W*E PASSED firemen fighting the fire, which had jumped Market Street and was beginning to devour the wholesale and financial district . . . As we left (the Call Building), the Grand Opera House, where a few hours before I had been listening to Caruso, was burning with explosive violence together with the back of the editorial rooms. . . .*

We started first to cover the fire I had seen start on its westward course from Third Street . . . We tried to make the fallen Brunswick Hotel at Sixth and Folsom Streets. We could not make it. The scarlet steeplechaser beat us to it, and when we arrived the crushed structure was only the base of one great flame that rose to heave with a single twist. By that time we knew that the earthquake had been but a prologue, and that the tragedy was to be written in fire. We went westward to get to the western limit of the blaze. JAMES HOPPER

56

On Market Street, at the *Call*, the situation was becoming desperate. The foreman of the pressroom reported that his boilers could not heat up because of lack of water. Then, a gas explosion in the sewer in front of the building sent an iron manhole cover flying through the air, forcing the type-setting machines out of commission once and for all. A few minutes later, it was realized that the offices of the *Call* and *Examiner* were in direct line of the fire and therefore couldn't be saved. The managing editors of the *Chronicle*, *Call*, and *Examiner* then held a meeting, resulting in the decision to ask for help from the Oakland *Tribune*.

AT THIRD STREET *we caught the starting-point of the fire. It had worked north as well as west, and the Call Building, the tallest skyscraper in the city, was glowing like a phosphorescent worm. Cataracts of pulverized fire poured out of the thousand windows. The* Examiner Building, *across the way, was burning. The Palace Hotel, treasured perhaps above everything by San Franciscans, was smoking, but was still making a magnificent fight. To the east the fire had gone as far as Second Street. There it had leaped Market Street toward the north, and was roaring, a maelstrom of flame, through the wholesale district, before the southeastern breeze . . . We went up toward the Hayes Valley district, in which heavy volutes of smoke announced another conflagration. . . .* JAMES HOPPER

From hillsides all over the city, the dome of City Hall could be seen through the clouds of smoke.

Left. The Palace Hotel, symbol for years of San Francisco's opulence and wealth, began to burn at approximately 3:30 P.M. Wednesday, April 18. Though its builders had taken great pride in making it "fire-proof," by Thursday it was a total loss.

Within six hours of the earthquake, the fire had swept over nearly a square mile of the south of Market Street district. All morning long, hundreds of people watched the efforts of troops and volunteers to prevent the fire from reaching the Palace Hotel. The hotel had a prodigious amount of water stored in roof top tanks and one basement reservoir, all filled by artesian wells in the basement. The staff spent hours trying desperately to wet down the hotel and keep the fire out. The attempts of the employees and the firemen finally had to be abandoned when the supply of water stored in the building was exhausted.

I CLIMBED *to the top of Potrero Hill to view the conflagration. On this hill many had assembled, and awestricken, with bated breath, were seeing the most awful sight they had ever beheld. It was now between nine and ten o'clock, and the business section, from Eighth street to the Ferry, a distance of perhaps a mile, was one vast furnace. A fierce and awful fire ate at the heart of the city and breathed up a suffocating black smoke. From eight, ten and twelve-story buildings, supposedly fireproof, flames issued at every window, and gushed from the tops like the blast from a rolling mill . . . It was too clearly apparent that San Francisco was doomed. That stupendous fire, and not a drop of water! Already the desert had followed the drought far in, where a great city stood.* F. O. POPENOE

While many of the older and more fragile buildings were being destroyed by high explosives, it was discovered that modern steel and concrete buildings were practically immune to anything except enormous charges. For example, attempts to blow up the Monadnock Building were futile. Located between the Palace Hotel and the *Examiner* Building, the structure, whatever its fire-resisting qualities may have been, was merely jarred by the concussions of the explosives.

Before noon, the firemen and troops realized that they would have to abandon their fight at Third Street near Mission. By this time, the military cleared Market Street of all spectators, allowing no one within the lines except reporters who were given improvised badges. Since the fire was several hours away, owners of many of the buildings within the lines criticized the military for their rigid adherence to emergency regulations, arguing that there would be ample time to salvage papers, records, documents, and other valuables. All the while, aftershocks could be felt over all of San Francisco.

The west's first skyscraper, the *Call*-Spreckels Building, caught fire at the top. The round windows in its dome glowed like so many moons before erupting with the heat.

During the first two days, few people realized that there was a narrow but safe way around the fire by means of the Embarcadero to the Ferry Building from which the boats were still running.

THOUSANDS *of dazed, half-frightened people moved about. The general drift was toward the ferry, but hundreds wandered without an aim. Three great columns of smoke hung over the south of Market district, two far down in the region of Second Street, one near at hand. The sidewalks and the streets were littered with broken cornices fallen from the skyscrapers, shivered plate glass, and castaway goods. Horsemen, fire-engines, trucks, automobiles, ambulances, delivery carts, and patrol wagons surged through the mass. Yet in the giant Emporium building the clerks were behind the counters methodically selling goods.*

At Sixth Street I looked down toward Howard two blocks away and saw a great hotel blazing like a furnace. At Fifth Street, another. At Fourth Street the fire had reached Mission, one block away. We came to Third Street. The tower-like Call Building loomed over us. Behind it the fire was blazing on Stevenson Street not one hundred feet away. Below the Palace and Grand hotels toward the ferry, tongues of flame showed on the south side of Market. With every block we advanced the crowd had grown denser. It was still half a mile to the waterfront. I gave up reaching the ferry. WILLIAM H. THOMPSON

Above. The fire along the San Francisco waterfront, photographed from a ferry boat on Wednesday, April 18. The ferries ran throughout the crisis, and thousands of people crowded aboard seeking the safety of Oakland and Berkeley. The Ferry Building, left, survived.

61

By one o'clock that afternoon, the fire had broken across Market Street in the vicinity of the *Call* Building on the southeast corner of Market and Third Streets. At that point, the flames veered with the wind, burning northward and westward through Chinatown, and there joined its destructive energy with that of a separate column of fire that had swept up from the lower end of Market Street and the waterfront.

The fire had consumed the *Examiner* Building earlier that morning and now threatened to destroy the *Call*. Next to the *Call* on Third Street was a three-story building in which there was located a shoe store, filled with a highly flammable stock of goods. The fire, as it rapidly made its way along Third Street, attacked that vulnerable structure which was soon a mass of roaring flames. The tongues of the flames leaped upward and destroyed the plate glass in the south windows of the fifth or sixth story of the *Call* Building. A group of soldiers and firemen standing near Lotta's Fountain were surprised to see the tall building on fire, for even while they spoke, thin ribbons of smoke could be seen streaming from openings far above. Soon, the structure's interior was ablaze.

Evacuees stand transfixed, watching their homes, schools, and offices burn.

In the background, the *Call* is almost hidden by smoke, while flames lick out of the windows of the Emporium department store.

THE FIRE *which had swept the wholesale district below Sansome, jumped Kearny Street and with a rattle of eagerness fastened upon Chinatown, with its carved balconies, its multicolored signs, its painted and gilded flimsiness. At the same time, doubling back, it came down Montgomery, San Francisco's Wall Street, and Kearny, fairly whistling down the deep, narrow corridors. By eight o'clock the Kohl and Mills Building and the Merchants' Exchange flamed like torches and the destruction of the business blocks of the city was complete.* JAMES HOPPER

The Wells Fargo Building, as well as other large structures, on Second Street was aflame. A short time before, the Grand Hotel had caught on fire; at the Palace Hotel, flames were shooting out all its windows at once; in the Mission district, where virtually the entire community was constructed of wood-frame structures, heroic efforts were being made to contain the fire. The intelligent use of the South-of-Market area's reduced water supplies, plus the hard, concentrated work of the residents seemed to have some early effect. There was more concern for the Mission district than any other part of the city, since as late as 6:00 P.M. on the first day, there was considerable hope the fire could be contained in the financial district.

THE FIRE had turned the flank of the fighters. The booming of dynamite at intervals of every few minutes told how desperate was the battle. The line of flames north of Market Street was eating into the blocks between Battery and Sansome. South of Market the flames had taken their victorious way to the westward beyond the line of the City Hall. The whole of the "Mission" seemed burning up. The red tide had engulfed the whole south side of Market Street from the Call building to the Majestic Theater opposite the St. Nicholas. All morning the air by a merciful providence had been still. Since noon a strong wind from the northwest beat directly into the teeth of the on-coming flames. . . .   WILLIAM H. THOMPSON

Lower right. The Lincoln School, Fifth and Mission Streets.

WE WENT up to Hayes Valley to examine the fire there. We passed the City Hall, the building upon which the city had spent six millions. It had crumbled at the assault of the quake and was now a ruin, noble with a beauty that it had lacked when entire. Here and there a massive column rose with its architrave, giving an effect of Babylonian splendor. Above the dome, divorced of stone, showed its naked skeleton, twisted as from some monstrous torture. . . .

The fire . . . already covered four square blocks and was sweeping toward the east. We went before it and stopped at the Mechanics' Pavilion . . . it had been used as a great hospital, but now, before the menace of the fire, the last patients were being transferred to the Military Hospital at the Presidio. We waited till the fire came. The immense wooden structure caught with almost explosive violence, and when we left the ruins of the City Hall were catching. We circled the fire south of Market Street again and found that it had reached Twelfth Street. At one o'clock we tried to report to the Chronicle Building. The Examiner, the Palace Hotel, and the Grand were burning fiercely by that time and we could not reach it. We started on another tour of the fires.

It was just about that time that the wind, which had arrived at the fire south of Market Street, had spread from Fourteenth Street down to the bay; and this immense frontage, driven by the wind, was moving south and east, the blocks literally melting before its advance. JAMES HOPPER

66

Grove Street in the Hayes Valley neighborhood, about 4 P.M. Wednesday. Except for a few small knots of people and an upright piano—the symbol of middle-class affluence and respectability—the area is deserted. While the downtown and "Ham-and-Eggs" fires raged, a temporary hospital was set up in the Mechanics' Pavilion across from City Hall. More than 300 people were brought here, as were valuable books and documents from threatened buildings elsewhere in the city. But on Wednesday afternoon Mechanics' Pavilion (the "Madison Square Garden of the West" and scene of a masquerade roller skate event the night before) had to be evacuated, the patients taken to Golden Gate Park and the Presidio's Letterman Hospital. The valuable papers were lost while, ironically, the buildings they were rescued from survived after all.

Early that afternoon the windows in the *Chronicle* and Crocker Buildings were noticed open. Firefighters feared that sparks raging south of Market as well as from the nearby Occidental Hotel would blow in, starting fresh blazes. But by nightfall, the two buildings were still intact and there was hope each would escape destruction.

All the downtown streets were now deserted except for sentries patroling Kearny between Market and California.

Accompanying *the proprietor of the* Chronicle, *we came upon the sentries. At first they declined to recognize the newspaper badge, but after a little parleying they consented to allow us into the lines, insisting the automobile not proceed any further. From Post and Kearny, we made our way to Montgomery Street where a very brief inspection convinced us that nothing but a miracle could save any structure in the neighborhood. All along Market, descending sparks were finding vulnerable spots. The* Chronicle *building, the new seventeen-story on Kearny, just finishing completion, and the ten-story structure on the corner of Market, Geary, and Kearny, were ignited in this manner. Later, a watchman employed by a clothing firm on Kearny told us that the roof of the ten-story* Chronicle *building, which was a temporary affair devised to protect the office staffs while two new stories were being added, caught fire around 3:00 A.M. and that the flames from it were communicated to the adjoining tall structures and from thence they spread southward.*

CHARLES YOUNG

All that night, April 18, the flames edged toward the Western Addition, one of the city's main residential sections. Meanwhile, Union Square was filling with refugees, most of whom brought whatever belongings they could carry. Virtually all these people had taken refuge there from various Kearny Street rooming houses. Overcome with fatigue, many of them were stretched out on the grass soundly asleep. A few were standing around a piano and sang songs. A reporter on the ensuing day described the impromptu concert as the only instance of artificial hilarity observed by him during the day and he ascribed it to an over-indulgence in wine. Meanwhile, there was no apprehension on the part of those in Union Square that they would have to abandon that open place, although their feeling for security was scarcely warranted by the appearance of their surroundings.

The fire was creeping westward, but there were no signs it would attack the mansions on Nob Hill or the new Fairmont Hotel, almost finished but not yet occupied. Chinatown, north of Union Square, was already burning, and everywhere the air was superheated, sparks and fire brands descending throughout the area. The St. Francis, as well as other buildings surrounding Union Square, were still untouched, although the hotel had long since been deserted by guests who had fled to other parts of the city.

Evacuees from the South-of-Market fire gathered in Union Square.

68

Up toward Nob Hill, beyond the St. Francis, the streets were lined with automobiles and other vehicles removed from the various garages. There was some evidence of fire-fighting; with wet blankets and whatever liquids or sand and dirt were available, they fought the shower of sparks as best they could. When property was saved, it was usually due more to a change of winds rather than their exertions. Some areas were totally deserted. In many cases, doors of houses and hotels were left ajar and whatever household effects had been removed to the sidewalks were simply abandoned.

Meanwhile, Hamilton Square, Alta Plaza, the cemeteries, the Presidio, and Golden Gate Park were already filled with large numbers of refugees stretched out on improvised beds and on the ground. The night was warm due to the fire's intense heat having overcome the city's natural tendency toward fog and low nighttime temperatures. Charles Young noted, "It may seem incredible, but on this awful first night of the conflagration, hundreds of persons, who had only to lift their heads to see that the city was encircled by a ring of fire, whose menacing front stretched several miles around them, slept as soundly as in their own homes."

Above, a refugee encampment in Jefferson Square. *Below*, Hamilton Square refugees set up temporary shelter. These first camps were very haphazard.

This family is camped out near Letterman Hospital on the military reservation of the Presidio. Similar scenes were to be recorded 25 years later when drought and dust storms drove the "Okies" to the golden land of California.

72

Left. Three fires can be seen in this dramatic view: The Market Street fire, South-of-Market fire, and the so-called "Ham-and-Eggs" fire in Hayes Valley.

Aᴌᴌ ɴɪɢʜᴛ *the city burned with a copper glow, and all night the dynamite of the fire fighters boomed at slow intervals, the pulse of the great city in its agony. When the sun rose, a red wafer behind clouds of smoke that were as crepe, the tidal wave of flame had swept three-quarters of it. Nob Hill, the Fairmont, the homes of the pioneer millionaires, Mark Hopkins's, with its art treasures were aglow, a ruby tiara upon the city. . . .*

Jᴀᴍᴇꜱ Hᴏᴘᴘᴇʀ

The next morning brought no change in the weather, indicating that hoped-for breezes which would arrest the fire's westward progress would not materialize. Everywhere west of the St. Francis Hotel people could be seen dragging or carrying whatever belongings they could. Vehicles were few and those who had them were charging exorbitant prices for their use.

Early that morning, a newspaper printed in Oakland arrived. It was a joint effort from the editorial staffs of the *Examiner*, *Call*, and *Chronicle* and passed out free excepting for enterprising newsboys who made a fortune from people in the outer districts hungry for news. Consisting of only four pages with seven columns each, this initial edition was devoted exclusively to the catastrophe. There were no advertisements and only the title indicated who had published it. The headlines and stories were not very reassuring on that April morning: "NO HOPE LEFT FOR SAFETY OF ANY BUILDINGS." The lead-in paragraph began: "San Francisco seems doomed to entire destruction." Naturally, there were many exaggerations, such as losses expected to reach billions of dollars and that twenty or more insurance companies would be ruined. But on the whole, there was an unusual amount of accurate information, thereby providing everyone with a realistic appraisal of the situation.

Such good journalism was surprising considering all the rumors in circulation: The entire Atlantic Seaboard had been engulfed by a tidal wave; Chicago was in ruins; the cataclysm was worldwide. The fact that Mt. Vesuvius had erupted five days earlier bringing death and destruction south of Naples was still fresh in everyone's mind. The assurances of Bay area geologists that San Francisco's earthquake was due to a fault and was not connected to any of these other events, real or imagined, was not likely to be believed by many.

All day Thursday the fire raged, and firemen, troops, and volunteers were doing everything in their power to prevent the flames from spreading toward the outlying residential districts. A steady stream of refugees was headed toward Golden Gate Park, while others sought to get to Oakland across the Bay. The fire had not reached the Embarcadero and the docks and Ferry Building were unscathed. But by late that afternoon, access to the Bay became more precarious and the homeless turned westward.

I WALKED down Market Street late in the afternoon of the second day. It was as if I walked through a dead city, not a city recently dead, but one overcome by some cataclysm ages past, and dug out of its lava. Fragments of wall rose on all sides, columns twisted but solid in their warp, as if petrified in the midst of their writhing from the fiery ordeal. Across them a yellow smoke passed slowly. Above all, a heavy, brooding silence lay. And really there was nothing else. Contortion of stone, smoke of destruction, and a great silence — that was all. JAMES HOPPER

The Call=Chronicle=Examiner

SAN FRANCISCO, THURSDAY, APRIL 19, 1906.

EARTHQUAKE AND FIRE
SAN FRANCISCO IN RUINS

NO HOPE LEFT FOR SAFETY OF ANY BUILDINGS

BLOW BUILDINGS UP TO CHECK FLAMES

WHOLE CITY IS ABLAZE

CHURCH OF SAINT IGNATIUS IS DESTROYED

MAYOR CONFERS WITH MILITARY AND CITIZEN

Looking west from the foot of Market Street. These displaced persons
are moving silently toward the Ferry Building.

This group of refugees seems content to set up housekeeping in the middle of Market Street.

77

While many of their fellow citizens did not realize that the ferries were still running, these San Franciscans huddled aboard the *St. Helena* bound for Oakland. *Far right.* A horse and carriage that might have rented for $3 on April 17 went for up to $50 after the fire started.

AT FOUR *this afternoon (April 19) a big cloud of smoke came over us—cinders as big as dollars began to fall and a shower of plaster dust. This frightened us. I packed three trunks and the boys carried them into the neighbor's garden. I wrapped a wet blanket around the band-box containing my new spring hat and hid it in a rose bush. We bought a four-wheeled cart from a small boy, made two two-wheeled carts out of it by using the pantry shelves for the body, loaded up one with food and the other with clothes and started out for my friends', the Towarts, sand lots on the other side of the Presidio. Van Ness avenue was full of people and movings—so full it spilled out into every vacant lot and side street. Going was difficult. Our cart broke down. I experienced the most terrible and senseless fear that this great mass of people, animals and things would stampede.*

MARY EDITH GRISWOLD

Early Thursday evening, residents of the Western Addition who climbed to high vantage points could see the flames still eating their way through the district south and east of Van Ness Avenue. The houses between Jones Street and Van Ness were all burning as well as all those on Clay, Sacramento, and Washington Streets. Confusion continued to reign. Owners of homes along the thoroughfares west of Van Ness were now uncertain what to do. Would the flames eventually reach them, too? Should they evacuate? Throughout the afternoon word was passed to open windows in order to avoid the destruction of glass from the concussions produced by nearby explosives.

To that point, almost no looting had taken place even though doors to homes were left ajar. Most people simply left their belongings and fled. But when efforts were made to remove personal belongings, curious selections could be seen: One man was tugging a sewing machine up one of the lesser grades of California Street while his wife, in tears, struggled after him carrying an empty bird cage; others were dragging heavy trunks, suggesting they were saving items other than clothes; some carried valuable paintings cut from their frames and carrying them rolled under their arms. Occasionally, residents would return to their homes in an attempt to remove more articles only to find a stern sentry awaiting them. Pleas were to no avail and no one was allowed in the area. The military sought to prevent looting as well as loss of life to adventuresome people. Furthermore, a plan was developed to dynamite certain buildings along the fire's route and secretiveness was imperative to avoid frantic confrontations with the owners and residents. Thus, sentries were inclined to treat anyone who argued with them as enemies. Such an attitude did not allay apprehension and rumors, but it did avoid needless deaths and injuries from both the fire and dynamiting.

On Thursday night, April 19, as the fire reached Van Ness Avenue, Colonel Charles Morris decided to blow up a number of buildings far enough ahead of the fire to make a clearing along Broadway, Franklin, and Gough Streets. Such a space, it was believed, would prevent the fire from spreading throughout the Western Addition.

HAVING crossed the broad avenue of Van Ness, which had been selected as a last stand by the fire department, the fire began to eat its way on several blocks west of Van Ness. Resuming operations on the east side of Franklin Street, we demolished all the buildings on that side of Franklin between Clay and Sutter, except for the wooden buildings between Pine and Bush. There was no order to our dynamiting. Instead, we blew up structures in which the existing conditions of wind and the encroachment of the fire demanded as most urgent . . . our work was carried out successfully, and by getting ahead of the fire on Franklin and demolishing houses between Franklin and Van Ness on the north side of Sutter, the fire was finally stopped.

While we were operating on Franklin, urgent demands for help came from the city authorities and fire department on Broadway and north Van Ness where the fire was out of control and threatening to outflank us . . . The wooden buildings at and near the southwest corner of Austin and Franklin caught fire, and the water supply being poor and the fire department tired out, the fire started to get behind us toward Gough Street. In order to head off the fire, in accordance with the preconcerted plan authorized by the mayor, I obtained authority from Colonel Morris to demolish the two wooden houses of flimsy construction and highly inflammable nature fronting on Gough. As the corner of Pine and Gough (southeast corner) was a vacant lot, and as the massive stone structure of Trinity Church on Gough, Bush, and Austin would check the flames, this demolition of the two little wooden structures would absolutely stop the fire coming up from Austin and Franklin. One of these wooden houses, the one next to Pine Street, was accordingly demolished, but before the other could be prepared, the fire department, which had succeeded in putting out the fire at Austin and Franklin, called for help at Sutter where the fire was getting out of control, having gotten out of hand while the fire department was working at Austin. This wooden building was the only house whose debris was not actually burned by the fire and its demolition was imperatively demanded by the conditions existing at that time, though a change in the course of the fire left its debris and the two adjacent houses unburned. CAPTAIN LE VERT COLEMAN

Meanwhile, a team was dispatched to north Van Ness to combat the fire working along the slopes of Russian Hill toward Van Ness south of Broadway. Beginning Thursday and continuing all day Friday, the military battled heroically. On Thursday, a group of soldiers had been so moved by the sight of the American flag waving from the roof of a house on Russian Hill that they had made an all out effort, utilizing mud and soda syphons, to save the house—"The House of Flag."

WE TRIED to head off the fire along successive lines and seemed on the point of success when another fire from the direction of Russian Hill swept back of us and I received instructions from the commanding general to cease operations in that section of the city. . . . COLONEL CHARLES MORRIS

By the next morning, April 21, the Western Addition was at last considered safe. The advancing flames south of the Mission district were stopped, but a rising wind forced the fire to turn northeastward from Russian Hill and engulf an area along the Bay which had thus far been spared.

The fire finally burned itself out along the waterfront north of the Ferry Building on Saturday morning. A day earlier, the fire in the Mission district had finally spent itself. While random fires still burned, no longer did any of them threaten the inhabitable areas of the city. Now it was time to take stock of what was left, begin the clean-up, and rebuild.

FOUR

. . . PEOPLE OF ALL NATIONS THROWN TOGETHER HIGGLETY-PIGGLETY.

THE EARTHQUAKE STRUCK, THE FIRES STARTED, and people fled, taking whatever for the moment seemed important to them. Rarely did the refugees consider food the most important item as they left their homes for the last time. Like as not, the things taken could not be explained to anyone but members of the family. Few had clothes other than what they wore; certainly, blankets and bedding, cooking utensils, and provisions were far down the list as trunks were packed, carts and wagons loaded, and escape from the destructing areas was accomplished.

There were people concerned immediately. Brigadier General Frederick Funston had made troops and Army vehicles available for firefighting and police supportive duties. Before 7:00 A.M., Mayor Eugene Schmitz met with city officials, including Funston, at the Hall of Justice to consider what emergency steps should be taken. He acted immediately to protect abandoned property by authorizing police and troops acting under supervision of the police to shoot anyone caught looting. Next, he ordered all establishments engaged in selling liquor closed until further notice.

AT THE Hall of Justice, in the midst of the Latin quarter, the Mayor, the Chief of Police, and their staffs together with the Citizens' Committee appointed immediately after the earthquake, were gathered in the basement. In the half-darkness, beneath the low-vaulted ceiling, they sat at long tables, their faces yellow in the light of the sputtering candles, and conferred in whispers. Near them was stretched a long line of stiff forms beneath white sheets. Out in Portsmouth Square, in front, the prisoners of the jail sat huddled in handcuffed groups. . . .
JAMES HOPPER

Schmitz then began drawing up a list of individuals he knew to be capable of handling specific problems. Disregarding previous political differences and animosities, the mayor selected able and experienced people, such as James D. Phelan, to head the action committees. While the mayor took action to supersede the powers of all city departments and commissions, he immediately delegated the authority to various committees under his direct control.

HALL OF JUSTICE

In the shadow of the ruined Hall of Justice, Portsmouth Square served as temporary police headquarters.

Of the more than 50 appointed to the Citizens' Committee, 25 came together at 3:00 P.M. in the Hall of Justice. By this time the fire was encroaching on the area and the dynamiting was going on in buildings in proximity to the meeting place. From the dynamite boxes in Portsmouth Square, the Committee moved up the hill to the Fairmont Hotel. There they worked through the evening outlining plans to save the rest of the city. At 9:00 P.M., they adjourned to meet early the next morning; however, flames claimed the hotel on Nob Hill during the night.

During the day following the earthquake, few people thought about food. The ravaging fire was on everyone's mind. But by Thursday, appetites were suddenly the new reality and the large numbers of people gathered in the parks and open places in the Western Addition had few provisions. The Committee established the procurement and supply of food as the number one priority, followed by clothes, bedding, and household necessities, then shelter, and finally provision for the future.

Lining up for rations in front of the commissary office at Fort Mason.

Milk being issued to families in the Western Addition.

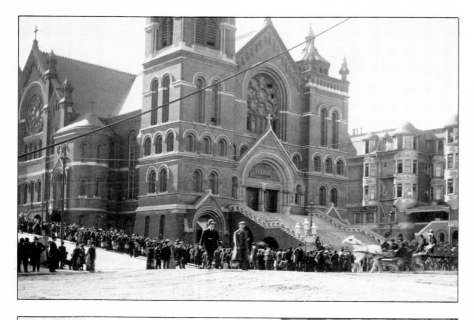

The wholesale warehouses containing the main stocks of food were in those districts gutted by the fire during the morning of the first day. And, naturally, the supplies of the retailers in the outlying districts were sold out almost immediately after the stores opened. Corner groceries were swept bare. In fact, when it was decided to requisition these food sources, there was nothing to requisition.

Rabbi Voorsanger headed the subcommittee on relief of the hungry. The rabbi was able to begin supplying the people in breadlines by noon on Friday, April 20, utilizing commandeered provisions. Some 35,000 loaves of bread were distributed by the committee that first day and arrangements were made to utilize what facilities remained to maintain a flow of food to destitute people.

Meanwhile, many of the outlying communities had organized their own committees to collect, transport, and distribute provisions. This well-intentioned practice benefited far fewer than would have been possible had they allowed their efforts to be coordinated by the Citizens' Committee. Fortunately, food supplies were pouring in from every direction. The Presidio, as well as other military installations, opened their stores and began distributing large quantities of bread and flour.

A long breadline snaking around St. Mary's Cathedral on Van Ness.

Nob Hill millionaire or factory worker, the fire had treated everyone as equals. On Jefferson Street everybody waited in the breadline regardless of social status.

86

Supplies were stockpiled in the parks, dispatched to relief stations all over the city, and distributed along the streets. But just why they weren't issued to men in Alamo Square is not known. These men don't look too happy about it.

88

At one of the bakeries on Friday there were two bread-lines, one five, the other eight blocks long. On Wednesday some of the grocers had thrown open their shops and bidden the people take what they needed. Others had asked famine prices; bread a dollar a loaf, canned goods a dollar a can, soda crackers five cents each. On these the soldiers descended . . . their goods were confiscated and distributed.

For three days money could buy nothing. Pauper and capitalist lined up together, basket on arm for rations or pail in hand for water. It was no forced equality. Class and wealth were forgotten in the common disaster, and each man spoke to his fellow on the street and lent a hand as he could. For the matter of that, as the banks were closed, no man was worth more than he had in his pocket, and many a prominent and prosperous citizen could reckon his wealth without the use of a dollar mark and might have starved as thoroughly as his poorest neighbor had food been at a price. JULIAN WILLARD HELBURN

The distribution of clothing and bedding was similarly undertaken. The military, the Red Cross, and the Citizens' Committee collected and effectively supplied the items needed by the refugees. Perhaps the styles were not up-to-date, nor did many articles fit properly, and many clothes had the suspicious appearance of obsolete military issue, but they were all sorely needed. The army received, stored, and distributed the goods, while the Red Cross established the need for aid. Here, the relief efforts of the surrounding communities were essential in supplying articles without the delays or discrimination later deemed necessary by the Committee.

Shelter was not of immediate importance owing to San Francisco's temperate climate and, the time being late April, the dry season had arrived, (although unseasonal rain did fall a few days after the earthquake). In the first few days, families and individuals settled in any safe place they could find, often securing the area by scattering their possessions around them. In this way, the parks and all open areas of the city were rapidly occupied.

As the days passed, more and more tents and tent-like structures blossomed among the refugees, as did shacks utilizing whatever boards or sheet metal could be found.

Facing page, above. Coffee and doughnuts or corned beef hash could be had in this make-shift restaurant in the shadow of the old San Francisco City Hall. *Below.* U.S. Army Relief Station in the Mission district.

Various modes of shelter were to be seen throughout the city. .
lean-to kitchen was built at Dolores and 18th Street. *Right.* Refugee
camp behind Letterman General Hospital in the Presidio.

Facing page. Golden Gate Park.

A tent encampment at the foot of Pacific Heights. Hilltop homes throughout the city fared very well as this photograph attests.

Tents in Lafayette Square, across Washington Street from the grand mansions of Pacific Heights. Many such contrasts and interesting juxtapositions were to be seen in the days following the fire.

THE RETURN *to the stone age was as complete as sudden. In a day the whole population was camped on the edges of a deserted and perishing city. Most of those whose homes remained abandoned them for the first few days, fearing either another earthquake or the approaching flames. And how gaily they took their destitution, these people! They built fireplaces on the sidewalks with the bricks of fallen chimneys.*

Just beyond the City Hall, in the very midst of the embers, a household had set up in a clever little shack of roofing-tin, gleaned from the ruins. It was inscribed broadly in charcoal, "Camp de Bum. Rooms to let — on the roof." In Golden Gate Park one tent was labeled "Hotel St. Francis," another "Camp Contentment"; a third drew smiles from everyone with the inscription, "God Bless Our Home." JULIAN WILLARD HELBURN

It was estimated that some 200,000 people had been left homeless by the earthquake and fire, of whom as many as 75,000 had managed to leave the city. Some lucky people were able to find space in the homes of friends and relatives, more were able to find rooms to rent, albeit some of them attics, basements, garages, and horse stalls. The army attempted to build barracks in Golden Gate Park to supply a maximum amount of space in a minimal time. This project was abandoned after only a few had been built because of problems of sanitation, permanency, and privacy. Tents provided a more intimate personal environment for their occupants and were considerably more useful: They could be erected quickly over a wooden platform, disassembled and moved easily.

WE ARE in the middle of an immense field (Fort Mason) — there must be thousands camping here — people of all nations thrown together higglety-pigglety. Our nearest neighbor is an Italian vegetable peddler and he has brought his entire family and household effects. When they went for the second load they left the baby here wailing an obligato to the accompaniment of a German fellow with a fiddle. Behind us sit a newly wed couple beside their trunk. The little bride is quietly weeping while her inexperienced spouse shows plainly that this is too much for one day. In the camps of the Latin races the men are doing all the talking, while among us English speaking people only the women are to be heard. On the top of the hill stood a bearded Italian waving a large chromo of St. Francis at the ever approaching fire, while he called upon the patron saint to save his city.

MARY EDITH GRISWOLD

Recently emigrated Japanese camped out on Fort Mason near old Gas House Cove.

Facing page. The Chinese were moved to a parade ground overlooking Fort Point on the Presidio. There was an attempt to keep them there long enough for their land in Chinatown to be overtaken by caucasian speculators.

97

During the disaster, the dead and injured had been accommodated in whatever way was possible under the difficult conditions. The dead had been largely ignored following the earthquake in efforts to locate injured persons in the ruins. With the fire, efforts were made to temporarily bury the dead with the intent of disinterring them for identification and permanent burial later.

The injured were cared for at various points, but the busiest improvised hospital existed for a short time at the Mechanics' Pavilion. Central Emergency Hospital was virtually destroyed in the earthquake; the staff and patients were then installed in the most convenient location which happened to be across the street—Mechanics' Pavilion. Located near City Hall, the Pavilion was threatened by fire on Wednesday, necessitating a withdrawal to temporary quarters in Golden Gate Park, and, eventually, all patients with available medical personnel were moved to the Presidio.

SEVERAL *of the large mansions, on the streets still secure from danger, opened hospitable doors, turning their livingrooms or their trim lawns into temporary hospitals. Ambulances and motors were employed in carrying the sick and the aged to places of safety.* CECIL CHARD

Facing page. Before fire attacked Portsmouth Square, a coroner's office and a temporary burial ground had been established there. After the fire, the bodies were exhumed and moved to sanctioned cemeteries.

99

MUCH OF *the efficiency of Funston's work was due to the automobiles. Nearly all in the city were requisitioned, and many of the owners volunteered to stay with them and drove them night and day in the government service. Autos brought the injured to hospitals and, as one hospital after another was reached by fire, bore the patients to safety. Daredevil chauffeurs tore through half-impassable streets with loads of dynamite. Orders were wigwagged from hill to hill as if the city were the desert, and from each hilltop were given to men in autos who hurried through the camps and streets, shouting the orders aloud and scoring them with chalk on blank walls and across the sidewalks. In two hours an order from headquarters could be known to everyone in the city. It was the speed and thoroughness of this service by which Funston averted a pestilence. From Friday to Sunday the danger was critical. Severe cases of contagious diseases had been found in the streets. The sewers were broken, there was little running water, and typhoid was imminent. To the stricken city, quarantine would have been the last straw. Prompt sanitary orders enforced with the rigor of martial law, prompt impressment of all able-bodied men to bring about sanitary conditions, saved the day.* JULIAN WILLARD HELBURN

Requisitioned automobiles drawn up on General Funston's lawn, Fort Mason.

RELIEF came with marvelous promptness. Physicians, nurses, medical supplies, poured into the city twenty-four hours after the shock; food, blankets, tents, a few hours later.

JULIAN WILLARD HELBURN

Remarkably, the number injured in the massive and swift destruction of the city was little more than 400. Many good medical facilities survived outside the fire zone and medical personnel willingly volunteered their services. Medical supplies not readily available in the city were easily secured from nearby communities.

The newspapers had managed to resume publication by utilizing facilities in Oakland and elsewhere, but telephone and telegraph communications were reserved for official use only. However, on Saturday, April 21, the post office, saved from the fire through the heroic efforts of employees, troops, and volunteers, resumed mail service. The city had established a registration system which allowed the addressee to be located whatever his circumstance. The difficult job was not made easier by the location of the post office in the midst of nearly impassable debris-filled streets.

The resumption of communication with the rest of the world had a morale-boosting effect. Of course, at no time during the fire was the city completely isolated from the rest of the world. But to those in the heart of the chaos, all ordinary forms of communications had vanished. When news of the disaster had been sent out, it was often terribly

exaggerated. Even the conservative reports of the calamity which were meant to be factual and reassuring wound up being misleading. As well as fact and rumor, pure imagination was used by editors in their desire to sell newspapers. In a Paris newspaper, it was reported that a tidal wave had engulfed the city. Some of the stories in the eastern newspapers were only slightly less fictitious. The result of these exaggerations was a flood of telegrams from anxious relatives and friends. Such demands overtaxed the telegraph companies, and deliveries were slow. This gave the impression that people who did not respond rather quickly were victims of the disaster.

An information bureau was established by the *Examiner* where a register was kept to aid in identification and location of missing relatives and friends.

IN CONNECTION *with the bread line, where the destitute gathered for free food, a most unique United States postal service was established. In a barrel was deposited a large quantity of scraps of white paper and sharpened lead pencils. Those desiring to send messages to their anxious friends provided themselves with these materials from the barrel, and wrote their notes as they slowly proceeded in the bread line. Near the end of the line another barrel was stationed. This was for the reception of the written messages. The message, written on one side, with the address on the other, and without stamps, were taken up by the postal authorities, and in due season each one of these bits of paper, with its few words to the anxious ones in the outside world, was safely delivered.* F. O. POPENOE

On Saturday evening, April 21, a major morale-booster occurred with the appearance of cable cars on Fillmore Street. All along the line, the cars were greeted with enthusiastic cheers which, according to one bystander, were an "expression of the instinctive recognition that the two widely separated residential districts that had escaped the flames were now bound together. The resumption of passenger traffic was regarded as a harbinger of the swift resumption of travel on all the lines of the city and the rejoicing was general."

THE DEPOPULATION of San Francisco had begun, ferry service was resumed, and Oakland was a seething mass of humanity. Here many of the most interesting features connected with the handling of the hordes of refugees were to be witnessed. The railroad was confronted by a tremendous task, as the fleeing multitude sought escape over its lines.

Upon the arrival of the ferry loads at the Oakland side, two lines would be formed—one, of persons going to localities within one hundred miles, the other of those who wished to depart, and the destination. Few questions were asked other than to inquire who you were, where you wanted to go, and how many there were in your party. A slip containing this information would be written out, handed to the person desiring transportation, and as the line progressed and he reached the staff of clerks at work, the slip was taken and a pass written out to correspond. F. O. POPENOE

Cable cars return to Market Street.

WHEN THE tents of the refugees, and the funny street kitchens, improvised from doors and shutters and pieces of roofing, overspread all the city, merriment became an accepted thing. Everywhere, during those moon-lit evenings, one could hear the tinkle of guitars and mandolins, from among the tents. Or, passing by the grotesque rows of curbstone kitchens, one became dimly aware of the low murmurings of couples who had sought refuge in these dark recesses as in bowers of love. It was at this time that the droll signs and inscriptions began to appear on walls and tent flaps, which soon became one of the familiar sights of reconstructing San Francisco.

> The cow is in the hammock
> The cat is in the lake,
> The baby in the garbage can,
> What difference does it make?
> There is no water, and still less soap
> We have no city, but lots of hope.

FIVE

MAKE NO SMALL PLANS

TWICE BEFORE, SAN FRANCISCO HAD BEEN DESTROYED BY FIRE. And, twice before, she had been rebuilt along the old lines and streets. The question on everyone's mind, even while the last few fires were being extinguished, was whether San Francisco would be rebuilt for the third time. During past decades, the city had taken pride in the historic tradition of triumphant resurgence. This had occurred so often during the Gold Rush years that a phoenix rising from the flames and ashes had been made one of the figures on the seal of the city.

The answer to the question was obvious. Now, however, it was hoped that broader avenues and fire-resisting building materials would make the new San Francisco as safe from conflagration as possible. The experience of the 18th of April had shown that no earthquake could destroy San Francisco. Its buildings withstood the shaking nearly as well as they had done in the great shock of 1868. But with water supplies cut off, fire could wreak disaster like no other force. No, San Francisco would be rebuilt, just as Chicago in 1871 after the great fire, and Galveston after the devastating hurricane and tidal wave in 1900.

While a large part of the population left the city during and after the fire, most of those who remained were bound together by the spirit of regeneration. For weeks, they worked and sustained strong feelings of the comradeship brought by the disaster. Social distinctions were temporarily swept away. Everywhere in the city outside the burned area, families of all classes cooked their meals on stoves brought out onto their sidewalks, following an order by the mayor to light no more fires in their houses. "Most of the servants have either run away or been sent away," wrote a correspondent for the Los Angeles *Times*, "and the people who get their own meals out of doors are among the best in the city. Cooking their dinners in the streets may be seen girls who have been educated at Stanford, Berkeley, Vassar, and Bryn Mawr." And the same correspondent reported that the most remarkable "of all the astounding leveling feats accomplished by the fire and earthquake" had occurred in front of the mansion of Adolph Spreckels on Pacific Avenue, where a daughter was born to Mrs. Spreckels behind some screens. "In the next block that same night a lost cat brought forth a litter of kittens."

Looking up Market from Sansome.

A panoramic view of the destruction photographed from Duboce Park. The dome of the ruined City Hall in Hayes Valley is on the left of Market Street. In the center distance is the Flood Building, and across the street is the gutted *Call*-Spreckels Building.

The Donahue Fountain, at Battery, Bush and Market, survived while everything else around it was destroyed. The monument, symbolizing man's industriousness, now pointed out his helplessness in the hands of nature.

During the next few days and nights immediately after the earthquake, civic leaders, architects, real estate promoters, and businessmen surveyed the scene. The burned-out downtown area represented over 2,600 acres, almost 500 city blocks or more than four square miles. The fire front had extended over a distance of nine miles. Insurance for just 300 of these prize financial district acres amounted to $250,000,000, although the actual property consumed was at least double that covered by insurance. According to the official statistics, 28,188 buildings burned.

The thirteen blocks that were not destroyed in the inner city had been saved because they were near enough to the water's edge for tugs to spray them with water from the bay. Two additional blocks on Russian Hill were saved by using water from a nearby service reservoir. The U.S. Mint was saved because of the efforts of its personnel using a pump and a deep-water well on the site. The post office on Mission Street also escaped the fire because it, too, had a deep-water well and was separated from adjoining structures by wide alleys.

The report of General Adolphus W. Greeley, commanding officer of the Department of California who had been attending his daughter's wedding in the midwest when the disaster struck, set the loss of life at 498 with 415 seriously injured. All in all, it had been a disastrous experience for San Franciscans. Yet, almost all accepted the earthquake as a natural phenomenon. The city, the people insisted, had never experienced the horrors of a raging blizzard or wind-

The United States Mint, built in 1875, was one of the very few buildings to survive the South-of-Market and downtown fires. A combination of solid granite construction, iron shutters, and round-the-clock firefighting of employees saved the building.

storm; floods, tornadoes, lightning, and extreme summer heat were unheard of. San Francisco could be made safe from earthquake and fire by proper construction of buildings and utilities.

Within a week of the earthquake, San Franciscans were restless to get the city back into some kind of normalcy. Actually, after a week of shared responsibility, self-interest moved businessmen and owners of property to salvage their burned-out wealth. While the Red Cross went about its work looking after the needs of the moment, Mayor Schmitz organized a Committee of Forty on the Reconstruction of San Francisco, consisting of San Francisco's most noteworthy men of affairs. By Saturday, three days after the earthquake, former downtown merchants were already seeking new quarters across Van Ness Avenue and in the Fillmore district where the flames had not penetrated.

The devastated city from Gough and Clay . . . a horrifying picture of destruction looking up Nob Hill, and toward downtown on the right.

Owners of these homes on Russian Hill stood on their roofs and beat out encroaching flames with wet blankets.

Above. Fillmore Street, looking north, near Bush one week after the fire. Fillmore Street became an extremely busy shopping district in the days following the fire and served the needs of thousands of San Franciscans living in the West Addition. Its pre-eminence was short lived, however, as the major downtown businesses preferred to relocate on Van Ness.

Facing page. This Fillmore Street laundry added a sideline—the selling of postcards and panoramic views of the recent disaster.

IN ALL *parts of the city thousands of men are now working clearing building sites, removing old bricks, hauling lumber and putting up temporary structures. Many of the leading retail stores have already opened for business on Van Ness avenue, and on other streets to the west of it. At present, Fillmore street is the main thoroughfare, principally because a cross-town electric line runs over it. But it is the opinion of the business men that as soon as conditions become a little more normal, business will again become concentrated in the old locations.* PACIFIC MONTHLY

In his *San Francisco: A History of the Pacific Coast Metropolis,* John P. Young wrote:

. . . the movement which made Fillmore Street for a time the center of activity was due to opportunities and opportunism, and not to the belief that it was the best place for carrying on business. An extraordinary occurrence had suddenly made a hitherto neglected thoroughfare available for the purposes of commerce. The bustle and activity which followed the establishment of new stores brought the purveyors of conveniences and amusements to the front, and very soon there was created a district in which all the features of downtown day and night life was reproduced.

The dynamiting along the east side of Van Ness, the widest street in the city, was done to prevent the fire from leaping across the broad avenue to engulf the Western Addition. The effort was largely successful, however the force of the charges shattered and blew out windows on the west side. *Left.* The street just below St. Brigid's Church collapsed after an underground water main broke.

After Van Ness was cleared it became the city's new retail center and many downtown businesses, including the Emporium, relocated along its length. The avenue's character was changed forever from a residential district to a commercial one.

Meanwhile, the Committee of Forty brushed the dust off a master plan for the city's improvement developed two years earlier by James D. Phelan and his Association for the Improvement and Adornment of San Francisco. At that time, the Association had employed the services of Chicago architect Daniel Hudson Burnham, then considered the leader of the city planning movement in the United States.

The shell of venerable Old St. Mary's Church, built in the 1850s, stands amid the rubble of California and Grant. It has since been rebuilt and the inscription on its clock tower still reads: "Son, observe the time and fly from evil."

W*HEN REBUILT, it will be one of the wonder cities of the world . . . Many thousands of people were rendered homeless, and although a great majority of these left town, there are yet encamped in the many parks of the city and along the hills, scores of thousands who depend upon the relief committees for shelter and daily sustenance.*

. . . People who shivered on the hillsides, under thin coverings; others who stood in long lines, awaiting the distribution of bread at the relief stations; others who went to headquarters to obtain tents and clothing, smiled cheerfully even in the hour of their direst want. On every side one may now see people wearing badges on which is printed the inscription, "Let's rebuild at once." JAMES D. PHELAN

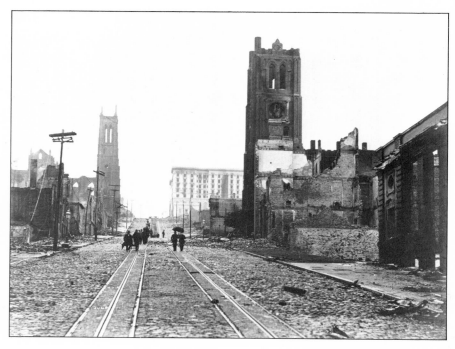

Looking east from the ruins of Chinatown at Washington near Powell toward the ruined dome of the Hall of Justice and the Ferry Building.

Some people preferred their own make-shift quarters among the ruins to the refugee camps in the parks.

Soldiers patrolled the deserted downtown streets, guarding the revealed safes of burnt-out office buildings and keeping away would-be looters.

121

THE PRESENT owners of the Fairmont (Hotel) were putting the finishing touches to the building when the 18th of one April rudely shattered the carefully laid plans. When the smoke had cleared away, a rejoicing people saw that the Fairmont had come through its baptism of fire structurally uninjured. The mansions which the bonanza kings had built on Nob Hill lay a twisted mass of stone, and iron, and smoldering wood, but the Fairmont cut the sky line with all the grace and beauty of its classic outline. The interior did not escape, owing to the inflammable material scattered throughout the building, and so all the decoration has had to be renewed.   FRANCIS BROWN

CHINATOWN had been burned out. It was a picturesque feature of San Francisco, and profitable as an attraction, but it was a center of more or less depravity; and it was unsanitary. The cry went up at once: *Abolish Chinatown; move the Chinese into a new part of the city, where they can have homes without being a menace to the community.* People did not question how this was to be done; it was a time when it seemed possible to do anything that was right and fine; for, as I have said, men had forgotten themselves.   RAY STANNARD BAKER

The view from Nob Hill overlooking the ruins of Chinatown and across to the surviving homes on the crest of Telegraph Hill. At the far right can be seen the facade of Old St. Mary's and beyond it, the Hall of Justice with its toppled dome.

Chinese Vice Consuls and representatives called upon General Funston at his Fort Mason headquarters. They were concerned—and rightfully so—that the Chinese in San Francisco would be deprived of their property. But less than two years later, Chinatown was thriving again, rebuilt just where it stood before the earthquake and fire.

After clearing operations began, investigators for the city discovered that buildings could be made safe with proper foundations. For example, even though they had been erected on earth susceptible to shock, the post office and Ferry Building structures withstood the earthquake because they had been given super-strong foundations. With new steel frames and other modern building materials, a businessman could build as high as he wished, or could afford.

And, as far as warding off fires were concerned, the city was in an especially good position. Geological surveys showed that the water supply of San Francisco was 36,000,000 gallons, considered excellent for a city of her size. A geological survey reported, "The failure to control the fire by reason of the crippling of the water supply was not due to the failure of the system outside the city, but the breaks in the distributing mains within the city which rendered unavailable 80,000,000 gallons of water stored within the city limits. These breaks occurred wherever the pipes passed through soft or made ground. No breaks occurred when the cast iron pipe was laid in solid ground, or rock."

The reputation Burnham established for himself during the designing of the "White City," the Chicago World's Fair of 1893, plus his brilliant plans for the Chicago lakefront area, brought him commissions from Cleveland, Detroit, and Washington, D.C. Burnham arrived in San Francisco in August 1904 in order to "conceive of a new city by the Bay" for Phelan's association.

Facing page. Looking west along Market Street, this photograph taken from the top of the Ferry Building shows the extent of the damage to downtown. The Ferry Building itself was damaged, and there was talk of tearing it down. But as it was a much-loved landmark and symbol there was a great deal of protest and it was repaired.

TWICE BEFORE has San Francisco been destroyed by fire; and twice before has she been rebuilt upon the old lines, her streets still narrow and her buildings still unprepared to resist a general conflagration. Now, however, it is to be hoped, broad avenues and fire-resisting building material will render the new San Francisco as nearly safe as human ingenuity can make her for the future. GEORGE C. PARDEE

Wagons hauling lumber head for reconstruction sites in the financial district.

Modern, steel-framed buildings rise from the ashes on Market Street. By 1909, twenty-seven surviving downtown buildings were restored, and seventy-seven new buildings were constructed.

A bazaar-like atmosphere developed along Market Street during the months of reconstruction. The Mutual Savings Bank Building is on the left of Market in this view, and the *Call*-Spreckels Building on the right.

Though the *Call* was severely damaged, it was rebuilt instead of razed. Now known as the Central Tower, the *Call* Building was remodeled in 1938; the dome was removed and six floors of offices were added.

The most important task to be done in the days after the fire was to rebuild the city's water mains. Work went on around the clock, regardless of the weather, and every able-bodied man was asked to help clean up and repair the city.

Free meals were provided for workers. These men are taking a lunch break at Crocker's Lunch Camp in Union Square.

Fear of new fires was always present until the mains were re-established and water pressure restored. The restriction against lighting cooking fires indoors was still in effect as this fire wagon answers an alarm on Post Street.

A well-earned drink at a fully functioning hydrant. The horses of San Francisco performed heroically during the clean-up; without them it could have taken years to clear the thousands of tons of debris.

The plan that finally emerged was entitled "The City Beautiful." In it were some of the most creative ideas to emerge in the early 20th century. Unfortunately, the plan did not take into consideration business or traffic surveys or economic needs. However, Burnham did suggest a rapid transit system, a forerunner of the BART system found in San Francisco and the surrounding area today.

Almost immediately, strong protest came from merchants and others who feared that the reconstruction of their businesses would be delayed by the uncertainties of Burnham's plans for relocating streets in the downtown areas. Burnham's original concept had contained such radical proposals as the one recommended in its "theory of the hills": ". . . each hill . . . should be circumscribed at its base . . . by a circuit road" with "contour roads" at various higher levels. Naturally, the business leaders were not concerned with the aesthetics of a unified city plan, but with the quickest way they could resume commerce in the most inexpensive structures laid out on streets that existed before the earthquake. In fact, among the ruins all around, the concept of "adornment" seemed no more than a fantasy.

Dynamiting near City Hall and along Market Street to bring down dangerous remains. The rubble was cleared and dumped as landfill in what is now the Marina district. Some humorists called the earthquake and fire the largest urban-renewal project ever attempted by God.

A few years afterward, the Civic Center concept did emerge as the one project salvaged from the Burnham dream. But in May and June of 1906, the only recommendation of Burnham's which was put into operation was the widening and grading of streets. And even in this case, it wasn't much of a change since all it meant was to narrow the sidewalks for "wider" streets.

The old Barbary Coast was located in the oldest section of the city, now known as Jackson Square. As well as housing respectable businesses, these brick buildings were the settings for some of the more unsavory activities that gave San Francisco its early reputation as a wild town. Many of the buildings had cast iron shutters designed to prevent fire from spreading from one tightly packed building to another. Note the steel buckled by the intense heat of the fire. The Hotaling Whiskey warehouse in the photograph to the right, next to the Columbus Paste Company, has survived to this day. Shortly after the disaster of April, 1906, this little ditty was heard around the city:

> *If, as they say, God spanked the town*
> *For being over-frisky;*
> *Why did He burn the churches down,*
> *And save Hotaling's Whiskey?*

It wasn't learned until years later that it was not an act of God that saved Hotaling's whiskey, but rather a group of industrious sailors who ran a firehose from the Bay two miles away in order to save these buildings of dubious reputation.

Extreme temperatures melted ironwork and reduced marble to useless chalk on California Street.

THESE ARE the days when the San Francisco Man-Who-Reads says strong and muscular words about certain correspondents and foreign editorial writers whose facts are based on his fancy. He reads of "The city that was," and says "Fudge!" and loses his temper when he finds San Francisco classed with Karnak or Nineveh. It's all mightly interesting reading—this twanging of the lyre on a one-tuned threnody for the lost city of the Golden Gate,—but as history it's mostly rubbish. San Francisco today bears about the same proportionate, pulsing relation to Nineveh that a Russian bomb does to Yorick's skull. This big western metropolis by the Golden Gate . . . is righting itself so rapidly and so gaily that rare old Phenix bird must be pluming and proud of its youngest chick . . . No wonder the loyal citizen says "Ski-doo!" to the calamity howler who discourses learnedly on earth-quake cycles, or figures that San Francisco's ocean-carrying trade must be divided hereafter between Guaymas and Sitka. Nineveh, Gadzooks!   CHARLES S. AIKEN

North Beach, then called the Latin Quarter, was primarily Italian. This neighborhood was a virtual loss from the fire that burned the area on April 20 and 21.

Before anything new could emerge, however, the ground had to be cleared. That task would have baffled Hercules, and according to Rufus Steele, cleaning out the Aegean stables was a child's task compared to clearing the damage for a new city. The final cost for removing the debris was approximately $20,000,000. Railroad lines were stretched across the downtown area for clearing purposes. Steam and electric cranes lifted the twisted steel beams and dropped them upon flat cars. Huge mechanical devices for shoveling and loading were invented and put to work. Steam and electricity were used in ways never before imagined. But when it came down to cleaning up the mess, it was the men, along with horses and wagons, that had to get the job done.

There were those allowed to sift through the debris and those who were not. Safecracking teams were closely supervised by the Army and the police. The opening of safes, still hot from the fire, took skill and caution — the paper contents could burst into flame when exposed to the outside air. Looters, however, were paraded to public humiliation.

Every able-bodied man in the city took up the task of clearing bricks from the streets. This view down Market Street shows the Flood Building in the center on the corner of Powell, and the *Call*-Spreckels Building behind the pole.

WORK! *I never have seen men work as they are working here. The need of work is so evident, so much is to be accomplished! Thousands of men are digging in the ruins, or sitting with dust spectacles chipping the mortar from fallen brick, or, perched perilously among the ruins, are attaching cables to twisted girders which the excited donkey-engines will straightway drag into the street. New steel rings to their hammers; wagons go forth dusty with debris to return with shining new lumber; cheerful wooden shacks spring up over night—with a little flag on top to let you know that there will be no capitulation! . . .*

RAY STANNARD BAKER

Before the reinstallation of the electric wires that powered the trolleys there was limited public transportation on Market Street.

Looking up Market Street, May 8, 1906. The city was hustling and bustling just as in pre-earthquake and fire days, despite the confusion of ruins and rebuilding.

138

THE EARTHQUAKE damage was inconsiderable. Every building on both sides of Market street stood against the earthquake.
The modern steel-frame buildings were unhurt, and that style of
structure stands vindicated. The city has to rise from the ashes of
conflagration, and not from the ruins of an earthquake. That it
will rise by the energy and credit of its own people is well assured.
Already it is threaded by temporary railroad tracks to carry off
the debris and clear the ground for building. . . .

CALIFORNIA STATE BOARD OF TRADE

All that remained of the once-elegant Palace Hotel, which cost
$7,000,000 to build, was a burned out shell. This photograph, perhaps
more than any other, symbolizes the tragedy of "The City That Was".

MANY OF *the largest buildings in town were not destroyed. The Call building, the Mills building, the Fairmount, the St. Francis, the Shreve building, the Mutual Savings Bank building, the Grant building, the Crocker building, the Kohl building, the* new Postoffice *building, the* Appraisers' *building, and many large warehouses and a score or more of other important buildings, although disfigured by fire, may be repaired and placed in good condition speedily.* PACIFIC MONTHLY

The St. Francis Hotel and the Dewey Monument in Union Square.

The Appraisers' Building.

A policeman surveys the damage in the main rotunda of City Hall. The building that took almost 30 years to build was constructed badly and was reduced to a skeleton in a matter of seconds.

No self-respecting family in the days following the earthquake would dare miss having its photograph taken in front of the "noble" ruins of City Hall.

SAN FRANCISCO—*let the name stand for the spirit of a great people—is not appalled, and one can already get a glimpse of the future through the smoke that bewildered it for a moment. While the world is asking, "What will they do?" they are doing it; are answering by laying the foundations, while yet the ground is hot, of a greater San Francisco than ever was dreamt in the more pleasant, but lesser days, of tranquility.*   F. O. POPENOE

The Hall of Justice.

146

The city jail.

147

The Tivoli Opera House on Eddy and Mason Streets. San Francisco's
ruins looked timeless—like the remains of a long-lost ancient culture.
The poet Will Irwin called them "the damnedest, finest ruins."

148

SAN FRANCISCO *knows its possibilities and it also knows its dangers. It knows the exaggerated earthquake stories that have reached the outside world. It does not wish to minimize the damage done by earthquake or deny the destruction by fire but it insists that it can accomplish what other cities have accomplished and it can, and will, out of its immense reserve energy, carve out a great and glorious future.* PIERRE N. BERINGER

149

150

OUT OF the horror and hardship of the earthquake and the fire, a new being has sprung into life and energy—the New, the Greater San Francisco—San Francisco Dauntless . . . More history has been lived in one short moon by the people of San Francisco than in all the period since '49. The old community has been obliterated spiritually as utterly as have the works of man. Doubtless, the old town had within it the seed of what it is today, but it had never pulled itself together for the great uphill task of accomplishing consciously and with intent its manifest destiny . . . Her hour of sleep and of content with what she had is passed and she looks now upon her future with a will to seize the opportunity which has been offered her by the erasure of all her old-time errors . . . JOHN GALEN HOWARD

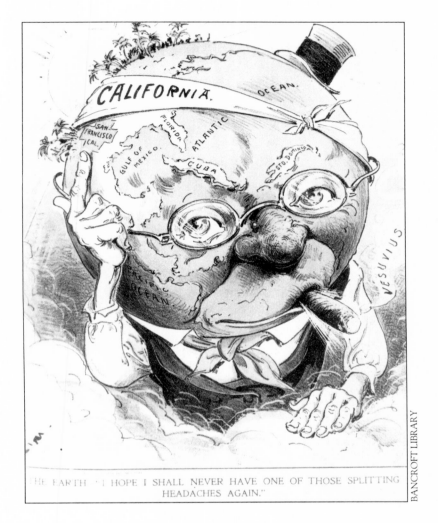

THE EARTH "I HOPE I SHALL NEVER HAVE ONE OF THOSE SPLITTING HEADACHES AGAIN."

Although badly damaged, the waterfront-warehouse district survived the earthquake and fire, thanks to the efforts of the United States Navy, and the San Francisco Fire Department. While these men battled the flames threatening the piers, ferries and small boats were still able to bring in badly needed food and medical supplies from across the Bay.

During the next two years, merchants and owners of real estate in the downtown districts feverishly went about their tasks of rehabilitating their fortunes. For the most part, they rebuilt on the same locations as before. The newspapers were on their side, insisting, "Visions of the beautiful must not blind us to the real needs of the city and the indispensable conditions of industries."

It is astounding to see how far San Francisco was able to rebound from the utter devastation of 1906 in such a short time.

Indeed, never did transformation crowd so closely upon the heels of devastation. In two years, over $100,000,000 worth of structures had arisen to obliterate the charcoal scars the fire had left. By April of 1908, one could stand upon the slopes of Twin Peaks and gaze across the majestic sweep of domes, towers, spires, and roofs which stretched four miles to the Ferry Building without any kind of a break whatsoever.

The style may be florid Victorian, but Rufus Steele captured the essence of the rebirth of the phoenix in *The City That Was*:

Pompeii ended when that city was destroyed, and since the discovery of its ruins dead Pompeii has been the sorrow of the world. The spirit of life breathed miracle breath upon the ashes of San Francisco, and lo! San Francisco arose to become the world's delight . . . Dollars are crude symbols. In this instance they were no full expression of what lay behind them. It is improbable that the power of money alone could have marshalled the new city. The men who emptied their coin sacks put other ingredients into the investment; labor did not smash all known building records in putting the town together for the simple sake of wages. The world felicitated San Francisco not so much upon the fact that it had put these millions into construction, as upon that which its spendings signified. The tall buildings expressed the vital ardor; the vital ardor was San Francisco's chiefest asset in the world's eyes. This vital ardor is something that might have shattered in the earthquake, and which did not shed a feather. It might have burned in the fire, and it did not even scorch. It is a real quality. It is neither an impulse nor a passion, for it does not grow cold and it does not consume itself. It is more than a state of mind, for a cataclysm did not serve to change it. A flame, it is like the perennial flame on the altar of Vesta. It is a sparking ignition set in the hearts of this favored tribe by the western sea, and its incense is faith. The San Franciscan cannot define it, but it defines him. And it has sustained a continuity over two broken years . . . The reconstruction of the City has literally no similar achievement to be found in all history. To San Francisco is granted the distinction of having done an unparalleled thing. The compliment, however, is not likely to evoke more than a passing smile from San Francisco, because the city has not finished its task.

The first bank to open after the fire was the Western National Bank located in the Flood Building on Market and Powell. Most of the bank records were lost, but a recognized depositor would receive a voucher which could be redeemed at the Mint for hard cash.

Most historians agree that there is no greater example of the destruction and replacement of a city than San Francisco. The first contract for a large building was signed, sealed, and delivered only five days after the earthquake hit. On that afternoon, the fires were still burning themselves out. Although there were no building materials on hand and few food supplies, San Franciscans were ready to go to work. While the first actual construction projects in the downtown area were devoted to converting burned-out wrecks into banks and loan and insurance offices, other projects were underway. For example, an expenditure of $5,500,000 was proposed to build a high-pressure water system second to none in the United States. An additional million was proposed to deepen the reservoirs of Twin Peaks, establish pumping stations near the Bay, build several fire boats, and construct one hundred reinforced concrete cisterns at strategic points throughout the city. Each of these cisterns would have the capacity to hold over one hundred thousand gallons each. Plans were also discussed to resurface city streets which had suffered enormous strains. Furthermore, a whole new sewer system was needed immediately. Public structures for the courts and civic offices were also absolutely necessary. Civic officials were scattered all over the city in private buildings, leased at taxpayers' expense. A $30,700,000 bond issue to cover all the needed structures was proposed in May 1906. A month later it was passed overwhelmingly.

Facing Page. The intersection of Third, Market, and Kearny. On the right, the hole where the *Examiner* Building had been; directly across Market is the *Chronicle* Building.

In the days during and after the earthquake and fire, just looking through the rubble could get you shot as a looter. But as the Army and the police relaxed the ban, souvenir stands sprang up all over the city.

156

Facing page. Looking up California toward the Fairmont Hotel in the early 1920s. The Stanford mansion across the street from the Fairmont was replaced in 1911 by the Stanford Court, which was remodeled in 1972. It is interesting to contrast this view with "The City That Was" on page 11.

The Metropolis Trust and Savings Bank (later the Merchant's National Building) on the corner of New Montgomery and Market, 1907. On the far right can be seen the framework of the new Palace Hotel.

The Sherman-Clay Building on the corner of Kearny and Sutter.

Looking south on Kearny toward the rebuilt *Call*-Spreckels Building; the new Sherman-Clay Building is on the right.

Looking up California from Market Street.

During the reconstruction period, San Francisco and her citizens came under attack by the eastern newspapers. They described how the city had been unprepared and how political corruption in city government had paved the way for that unpreparedness. In fact, many correspondents with a bit of eastern snobbishness ridiculed the values and ethics of "westerners." The average San Franciscan was indifferent to such absurd attacks. He was much too busy "doing things" to pay much attention to what others had to say about him. So, Benjamin Ide Wheeler, president of the University of California at Berkeley, felt it only fair to offer a vigorous defense:

More than in any great city of the continent men here are trained by experience to look out for themselves and are not much inclined to the task of being their brother's keeper. If the prevalence of personal independence is one of the hindrances to the city's corporate development, it must also be admitted that it constitutes one of the peculiar charms of the city's personality. She is a breezy city, fond of beauty, sport, and song, and withal intensely human—without regrets, so that her demurer, if not purer, eastern sisters often fail to understand her quite. Those who understand her love her, with all her whims and vagaries.

Facing page. The Monadnock Building, under construction at the time of the earthquake and fire, withstood attempts to dynamite it.

The Hall of Justice on Portsmouth Square was rebuilt without its dome; it was torn down in the 1960s to make room for the Holiday Inn.

In 1915, the nations of the world joined together in a major international exposition to share the things of which they were most proud. Amid all the thousands of displays, everyone agreed that the greatest exhibit was the city, San Francisco itself. Everyone marveled at how a city whose heart had been burned out only nine years before now showed hardly a trace of the wound. When visitors from all over the world poured into the city, they found a metropolis risen from the ashes.

In 1909, after three years of rebuilding, the city dusted off plans for an international fair begun in 1904. In 1915, San Francisco hosted the nations of the world at the Panama-Pacific International Exposition, celebrating the opening of the Panama Canal. Surrounding all the colorful and imposing displays was the greatest exhibit of all, the city itself. The Palace of Fine Arts, designed by Bernard Maybeck for the celebration, still stands, an enduring monument to the resurrection of the "City That Was."

BIBLIOGRAPHY

Books

Bronson, Edward, *The Earth Shook, The Sky Burned.*Garden City, NY: Doubleday, 1959.

Coffman, Jerry L., and Carl A. von Hake, *Earthquake History of the United States.* Washington, DC: Government Printing Office for the National Oceanic and Atmospheric Administration, 1973.

Gilbert, Grove Carl, et al, *The San Francisco Earthquake and Fire of April 18, 1906.* San Francisco: San Francisco Historical Publishing Co. Reprint of 1907 report by the U.S. Geological Survey.

Greeley, Major General Adolphus W., "Appendix A: Earthquake in California, April 18, 1906," *Annual Report of the War Department 1906.* Washington, DC: Government Printing Office, 1906, pp. 91–253.

Kennedy, John Castillo, *The Great Earthquake and Fire,* San Francisco, 1906. New York: Wm. Morrow & Co., 1963.

Laval, Jerome D., *Images of an Age,* San Francisco. Fresno, CA: Graphic Technology Co., 1977.

Lawson, Andrew, *The California Earthquake of April 18, 1906,* 2 volumes. Washington, DC: Carnegie Institution, 1969.

Olmsted, Roger, and T. H. Watkins, *Mirror of the Dream: An Illustrated History of San Francisco.* Oakland, CA: Scrimshaw, 1976.

Russell Sage Foundation, *San Francisco Relief Survey.* Kennebunkport, ME: Milford House, 1974 (reprint of 1913 ed.)

Thomas, Gordon, and Max Morgan, *The San Francisco Earthquake.* New York: Stein and Day, 1971.

Periodicals

Aiken, Charles Sedgwick, "San Francisco—One Year After," *Sunset,* April 1907, pp. 501–512.

_____, "San Francisco's Plight and Prospect," *Sunset,* June-July 1906, pp. 13–22.

_____, "San Francisco's Upraising," *Sunset,* October 1906, pp. 301–311.

Anderson, Van W., "The Story of the Bulletins," *Pacific Monthly,* June 1906, pp. 774–745.

Armes, Wm. Dallam, "The Phoenix on the Seal," *Sunset,* June-July 1906, pp. 113–115.

Austin, Mary, "The Temblor," *Out West,* pp. 497–506.

Baker, Ray Stannard, "A Test of Men," *American,* November 1906, pp. 81–96.

Beringer, Pierre N., "The Destruction of San Francisco," *Overland Monthly,* May 1906, pp. 391–406.

Branner, J. C., "The California Earthquake from the Geologist's Point of View," *Pacific Monthly,* supplement, 1906, pp. 6–10.

_____, "Geology and the Earthquake," *Out West,* pp. 513–518.

Brown, Francis, "A Nob Hill Anniversary," *Sunset,* April 1907, pp. 70–73.

California State Board of Trade, "The Rebuilding of San Francisco," *Pacific Monthly,* supplement, 1906.

Chandler, Katherine, "Saving Mission Dolores," *Sunset*, June–July 1906, pp. 115–116.

Chard, Cecil, "The Aftermath of the San Francisco Earthquake," *Pall Mall*, August 1906, pp. 267–270.

Cohen, Edgar A., "With a Camera in San Francisco," *Camera Craft*, June 1906, pp. 183–194.

Cowles, Paul, "What Really Happened," *Out West*, June 1906, pp. 477–497.

Currie, Barton W., "Some Reconstruction Figures," *Sunset*, October 1906, pp. 312–318.

The Destruction of San Francisco," *The World To-Day*, June 1906, pp. 560–568.

Douglass, Marshall, "The Destruction of San Francisco," *Pacific Monthly*, June 1906, pp. 625–633.

Duryea, Edwin, Jr., "A Better City," *Overland Monthly*, September 1906, pp. 109–128.

Dutton, Arthur H., "The Triumph of the Automobile," *Overland Monthly*, September 1906, pp. 145–154.

Emerson, Edwin, Jr., "Handling a Crisis," *Sunset*, June–July 1906, pp. 23–35.

_____, "San Francisco at Play," *Sunset*, April 1907, pp. 319–328.

French, Harold, "How the Mint Was Saved," *Sunset*, June-July 1906, pp. 116–117.

_____, "How the Red Cross Society Systematized Relief Work in San Francisco," *Overland Monthly*, October 1906, pp. 195–206.

Griswold, Mary Edith, "Three Deep Adrift," *Sunset*, June-July 1906, pp. 119–122.

Harriman, E. H., "San Francisco's Experience," *Sunset*, June-July 1906, pp. 37–41.

Helburn, Julian Willard, "The Quickening Spirit," *American*, July 1906, pp. 294–301.

Hopper, James, "Our San Francisco," *Everybody's*, June 1906, pp. 760a–760h.

Howard, John Galen, "The Rebuilding of the City," *Out West*, pp. 532–536.

Hudson, James J., "The California National Guard in the San Francisco Earthquake and Fire," *California Historical Quarterly*, Summer 1976, pp. 137–149.

Inkersley, Arthur, "An Amateur's Experience of Earthquake and Fire," *Camera Craft*, June 1906, pp. 195–200.

_____, "What San Francisco Has to Start With," *Overland Monthly*, June-July 1906, pp. 458–483.

Jennings, Rufus P., "Organization in the Crisis," *Out West*, pp. 519–525.

Jordan, David Starr, "Cause of the Great Earthquake," *Cosmopolitan*, August 1906, pp. 343–351.

Laffler, Henry Anderson, "My Sixty Sleepless Hours," July 1906, pp. 275–280.

Leuschner, A. O., "The Scientific Aspect of the California Earthquake," *Pacific Monthly*, supplement, 1906.

Miller, Mary Ashe, "My Own Story," *Pacific Monthly*, August 1906, pp. 229–234.

Pardee, Geo. C., "Will San Francisco Be Rebuilt?" *Pacific Monthly*, 1906, pp. 647–648.

Phelan, James D., "The Future of San Francisco," *Out West*, pp. 537–538.

_____, "The Present Situation," *Pacific Monthly*, June 1906, pp. 649–650.

Popenoe, F. O., "The San Francisco Disaster," *Pacific Monthly*, June 1906, pp. 727–736.

Rea, Irvin, "The Reconstruction of San Francisco," *Pacific Monthly*, June 1906, pp. 737–739.

Smythe, William E., "The Ennoblement of California," *Out West*, pp. 539–541.

Steele, Rufus, "The Spread of San Francisco," *Sunset*, June 1907, pp. 109–122.

Strong, Elizabeth Haight, "San Francisco's Upbuilding," *Sunset*, December 1906, pp. 115–118.

Thompson, William H., "Watching a City Perish," June 1906, pp. 592–596.

Voorsanger, Jacob, "The Relief Work in San Francisco," *Out West*, pp. 526–531.

Walcott, Earle A., "Calamity's Opportunity," *Sunset*, August 1906, pp. 151–157.

Wall, Louis Herrick, "Heroic San Francisco," *Century*, August 1906, pp. 579–593.

Wells, William Bittle, "Views," *Pacific Monthly*, June 1906, p. 749.

Wheeler, Benjamin Ide, "The Future of San Francisco," *Century*, August 1906, pp. 630–632.

Wood, Charles Erskine Scott, "Impressions: There Is No Real Help But Self Help," *Pacific Monthly*, June 1906, pp. 750–752.

Wood, W. D., "San Francisco's Optimism and Reasons For It." *Pacific Monthly*, June 1906, pp. 737–739.

INDEX